To Rex Minton —
From One Horseman to Another —
Hold a Tight Rein!

R. Lewis Bowman
1999

Bumfuzzled

confused; assembled without order or reason; discombobulated

1

First Edition

Library of Congress Catalog Card Number 95-94750

Published by R. Lewis Bowman

Printed by Copper Queen Publishing Inc.
P.O. Drawer 48 Bisbee, Arizona, 85603
Phone 520-432-2244 Fax 520-432-2247

ISBN# 0-9646758-2-X

Printed in the United States of America

TABLE OF CONTENTS

BOLD PRINT - QUIPS AND PHASES
ITALICIZED WORDS - GLOSSARY

Cover Photo - The author, R.Lewis Bowman, at the
launching of Junior Rodeo in Dallas,
Texas, in 1929.

THANKS TO THE CREW

B.J. Kuykendall	editor, cartoonist
Tom Kuykendall	computer, layouts
Tammy Sue Smith	free hand illustrations
My Family	history, reviews, encouragement and support
Fannye Lovelady	CTA material, photos
Margie Greenough Henson	history, photos
Dedrick Wilson	proof reading
Karen Straub	proof reading
Anne Marie Moore	information
Cordelia Lewis	history
Alice Gayler	history, photo
Gloria Willson	photo
Copper Queen Publishing, Inc.	printers, distributors
National Cowboy Hall of Fame	history
Pro Rodeo Hall of Fame	history, material

Reviews and Quotes

Gov. Jack Williams   Gov. Rose Mofford

Rex Allen   Jack Nelson

Hon. Polly Rosenbaum

Family, Friends and Acquaintances   livestock brands

PREFACE

This book is dedicated to my father, Dick Bowman, his older brothers, Ed and Walt, his younger brothers, Everett and Skeet, and all the other cowmen and cowboys that I have had the privilege of growing up with, and working with, all of my life.

This compendium of cowboy quips and phrases presented in the cowboy's manner of speech has come, in part, from my lifetime association with these fellas; the greatest people in the world...honest, caring, unsurpassed outdoorsmen. These are some of the ones who helped make the west. They settled it, homesteaded it, improved it, took care of it; made it the best it could be for me and my successors and everyone else concerned.

Sadly, the old time cowboy wit and philosophy, and the style in which he delivered it, is a dying thing. I have attempted to preserve a small part of it, and included a little bit of history from my personal collection of photographs, for whatever it may be worth.

R. Lewis Bowman

Bisbee, Arizona

INTRODUCTION

Will Rogers once said; "Those were the great old days. Darn it, any old days are great old days, even the tough ones. After they are over, you can look back with great memories."

R. Lewis Bowman has captured many of these memories by depicting the humor and unique sampling of an incurable way of life; the life of the rancher, the cattleman, the cowboy. The life that is part of Mother Earth.

The author's family and others like them, accepted the challenge to uphold the true American spirit. For generations, these dedicated human beings defied all odds, and in so doing, have created a composition that reflects the code we should all live by.

Please join us as we turn back the clock, recalling some of those "great old days" and authentic western legends.

B. J. Kuykendall

Rucker Canyon, Arizona

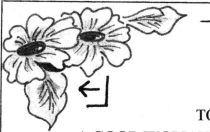

TO **BARBIE**
A GOOD WOMAN IS HARD TO COME BY....

BARBARA BUTLER BOWMAN
1922 - 1994
Those forty-six and a half years wouldn't have amounted
to much without you, Sugar.

**A HALF-ASSED PLAN IS BETTER THAN
NO PLAN AT ALL....**

Old Settlers

DON'T FORGET WHERE YA CAME FROM

The homestead of George W. Lewis, my great-great-grandfather at Weed, New Mexico, about the turn of the century.

FJL

There are not many descendants remaining from that era, so I was unable to identify these cowboys. Grandpa Lewis built this house, mainly with his hands and an axe, soon after his arrival to the area on August 19, 1884.

Great-great-grandmother Lewis became the mid-wife for

their rural area. She delivered my father, four of his brothers, plus many other of the Lewis grand-children in this house. A sister, Maudie Campbell of Globe, Arizona, was born at Hope, New Mexico. She is the last survivor of her family.

Grandma Lewis was noted for her ability and diligence as a mid-wife. She traveled horseback, riding side-saddle, carrying her sachel of equipment as far as forty or fifty miles to attend to anyone who called her.

Grandpa Lewis' log house still stands today and is kept in good repair by his grand-daughter, Cordelia Lewis, age ninety-six, of Weed. Cordelia recently commented, "I was born in 1899 in this house. If I can make it four more years I can 'crow' that I took care of my grand-parents home for a hundred years. I'm sure my niece, Jane Lewis Schafer, who has been my 'partner', will do the same when I'm done."

The log house and much of grandpa Lewis' ranch, have remained in the Lewis family for one hundred and eleven years. The seventh generation is now represented there. It seems like it could be concluded that six generations of the Lewis family succcessfully operating this ranch, is testimony to adequate stewardship of these lands. At least there have surely been a lot of taxes,baby shoes and school books purchased from the care of this ground!!!

George and Mary Lewis with eight of their eleven
children at the Lewis Homestead in Weed, New Mexico,
about 1905.

Grampa Lewis came from Georgia, to Texas, to Weed,
New Mexico, in 1884. His third generation descendants
still own his original homestead.

COWBOYS NEVER RETIRE.... THEY JUST KEEP REACHIN' FOR A *DEEPER SEAT*

George W. Lewis, at age ninety-one.

THERE'S NO WAY YA CAN POSTPONE GETTIN' OLDER

THE BEST THING ABOUT MINDIN' YOUR OWN *RAT KILLIN'* IS YOU SELDOM RUFFLE ANYONE ELSE'S FEATHERS

Lewis and Lottie Peach, my maternal grandparents, operated the hotel and cafe in Columbus, New Mexico, in 1916 when the revolutionary, Pancho Villa, from Mexico, raided the town. Grandpa and Grandma sought safety under their bed, and things seemed to be going all right until the urge of one of Grandpa's daily habits took over. It was evening at which time he always enjoyed a piece of pie. He insisted that Grandma get up amidst the hail of rifle fire and get his pie. I'm told that Grandpa went without his pie that day!

℘

WHEN YER ON CRUISE CONTROL... DON'T FORGET WHERE THE BRAKE IS....

My grandparents, Tom Bowman, the "Shotgun Rider," and Susan Bowman, "Teamster," in the grand entry of the Prescott Arizona Rodeo in 1925. They made the trip from Safford, Arizona, to the "show" in their Ford car in three days, a distance of about three hundred miles. (Had to patch a tire or two enroute!)

THERE'S NO SUBSTITUTE FOR COMMITMENT

W.T. "Tom" Bowman and his family at his general store in Hope, New Mexico in 1896. From the left are Tom, his sons Walter, John, Ed, Dick, Tom's wife Susan Lewis Bowman, Susan's brother Dave Lewis, and Dave's wife Fronie.

TOS

Tom, my grandfather, came from Missouri to Weed, New Mexico in 1884. Here he met Susan Lewis and they were married a year later. Five of their children were born at Weed. Grandpa did whatever he could to feed his family. He raised cattle, horses and mules and established this General Store at Hope, New Mexico.

When the store burned down in 1907, Grandpa loaded up two wagons and moved his family to Big Springs, Texas. He went into the freighting business, hauling mostly for the local lumber yard. Jess Willard, who later became the World Heavyweight Boxing Champion, from 1915 to 1919, worked for Tom for a time.

Tom and Susan's number three son Walt, at about age twenty, came home to the family from his cowpunching tours and got a job at the lumber yard. His job was unloading ninety-six pound sacks of cement from railroad cars. Being paid by the sack, he would carry four sacks at a time from the cars to the warehouse without any mechanical or human assistance. Uncle Walt said it was the best paying job he ever had in his life!

YOUTH HAS ITS OWN NATURAL BEAUTY

Tom Bowman at Safford, Arizona in 1915, with his son, Skeet, daughter Maudie, wife Susan, son Dick, daughter-in-law Louise, and son Ed.

From Big Springs, Texas, the Bowman family moved to Clifton, Arizona in 1913. Tom worked for the mining company a couple of years teaching the "Mule Skinners" how to drive mule-drawn ore wagons. He retired at Safford, Arizona, in 1917, where he opened a part time refreshment stand on the city's main street.

AN ANGEL ON EARTH

Susan Bowman, my Grandmother

Grandmother had seven children: Ed, John, Walt, Dick, Everett, Skeet and Maudie. She had fourteen grand-children. All felt they were the "apple of her eye." The same feeling was held by everyone who knew her, being either relative or friend. With her sincere concern for everybody, she was something "special." Guess you can tell I really loved my grandmother Bowman... so did everyone else who had the good fortune of knowing her.

AN OLD COWBOY HAS ONLY THREE TRUE FRIENDS LEFT: AN OLD WIFE, AN OLD DOG, AND READY CASH

Tom and Susan Bowman, at Tom's refreshment stand in Safford, Arizona, in 1917. Grandpa kept himself content in his retirement years entertaining the public and earning some income.

I'm sure this phase of life was not quite as exciting as the preceeding years, but my grandpa was not a believer in "idleness." Guess he was afraid if he sat around he'd "rust."

IF YA DON'T USE IT... YA LOSE IT

Tom Bowman and Darkus at the refreshment stand. Darkus was an exceptional pet, understanding and obeying any command Tom gave him.

Each day at lunch time, Darkus would take a nickle (5 cents) given to him by his master, to the butcher shop about a block down the street. Dropping the nickle at the butcher's feet, Darkus would wait for Tom's friend to wrap up some fresh beef for him. Darkus always took this lunch package back to Tom and waited for permission to open it and eat.

SURE HAS BEEN TOUGH NEVER
HAVIN' SEEN A DINOSAUR....
BUT MOST OF US HAVE MADE IT OK....

Mom and Pop

DON'T WALK WHEN YOU CAN RIDE

My parents, Dick and Clara Bowman in 1947.

Mother was born in Illinios. In 1902, at the age of five, she moved via covered wagon to Columbus, New Mexico with her parents. Her father, Lewis Peach, was a building contractor and he had obtained jobs in Chihuahua, Mexico. Things were going well for them until Pancho Villa, the Mexican revolutionary, went on the "War Path" in northern Mexico in 1915. Grandpa then settled at the border town of Columbus where he operated a cafe and hotel. He also homesteaded eighty acres near the town.

$\mathcal{WB}$

IT PAYS TO STAND ON YOUR OWN TWO FEET

Clara Bowman, my mother, putting Chum, the Hook and Line Ranch pet blacktail deer, through his tricks in 1948. Chum was a *DOGIE* that the ranch folks raised on a nanny goat. A mountain lion had killed Chum's mother when he was just a few days old. Uncle Ed Bowman was horseback when he found the lion kill and Chum nearby at the point of starvation. Ed carried the baby home in front of him in the saddle and grafted him on to the nanny goat. Chum turned out to be a friend of everyone. He must have grown up thinking he was a goat, as he lived to a ripe old age, content among the goats that were kept around the ranch house for the purpose of roping practice.

ALL THE SECURITY A MAN HAS IS WHAT HE CARRIES AROUND IN HIS OWN SHOES

David R. "Dick" Bowman, my father, as a private in the U.S. Army during World War I. Dad claimed he was where the bullets were the thickest during his days at war. He drove an ammunition wagon with a four-mule *HITCH* through France to the front lines during nighttime hours. One of his draft mules was a solid white color and Dad said he might have brought the idea of camouflage to his unit. Every time he found a water hole large enough, he would throw the white mule down in it and cover it with mud so that it wouldn't be so visible to enemy fire.

LEADING BY EXAMPLE RATHER THAN COMMAND CAN PRODUCE GREATER RESULTS

THE SQUEAKIN' WHEEL GETS THE GREASE

In 1916 Dick Bowman was employed as a truck driver by the U.S. Army at Columbus, New Mexico. General John J. Persing was in pursuit of the renegade Pancho Villa in Mexico. Dick's job was hauling supplies for the Army troops.

Dick met Clara Peach at Columbus, where her father Lewis Peach operated a hotel and cafe and served as Justice of the Peace. Dick and Clara were married prior to his departure to France with the U.S. Army during World War 1.

MOST COWBOYS ARE TOUGHER'N A BOOT AND STILL SOFT AS PUTTY

Dick Bowman, 8 Cowboy

After his service in France with the U.S. Army during World War I in 1918, Dick Bowman, my father, punched cows for his oldest brother Ed on his Steeple 8 Ranch at Hawk Canyon, ten miles south of Old San Carlos, Arizona.

NO USE HURRYIN' WHEN EVERYTHING'S UPHILL

Dick Bowman, driver of the Globe to Payson, Arizona mail stage in 1919.

Dick worked for See and Valentine in Globe, Arizona, driving the mail stage from Globe, over Roosevelt Dam to Payson, Arizona, some eighty miles all up hill. The schedule called for transporting mail and passengers up one day and back the next. Roads weren't much in 1919, nor were the vehicles. Dick reported, "You never knew how long it would take to make the round trip. In rainy weather it could take as much as a week." (Ed. note: the same one way trip today, seventy-six years later, over an all-weather road takes less than two hours.)

IF IT AIN'T BROKE... DON'T FIX IT

Dick and Ed Bowman working on Ed's Model T, his
first car.

Dick Bowman took a job with the U.S. Indian Service at
Old San Carlos, Arizona, in 1923 after driving the Globe to
Payson mail stage and the Globe to Lordsburg, New
Mexico, "Pickwick" stage for about four years. His work
included a "jack-of -all-trades" which he parlayed into self-
made achievements in electrical, mechanical and hydro-
logical engineering.

HARD WORK IS THE BACKBONE OF PRODUCTION... PRODUCTION IS THE KEY TO SUCCESS....

Dick Bowman's first car, a Star.

From the U.S. Indian Service, Dick transferred to the U.S. Bureau of Reclamation as a supervisor of electric transmission power line construction down the Colorado River below Davis Dam from 1950 to 1952. From there he supervised parts of the All American Canal from Yuma, Arizona, to Coachella, California.

Here he retired from Civil Service employment after thirty-eight years of service. He spent his active retirement years at Scottsdale, Arizona.

DON'T TELL ANYONE YOU WANT TO BE A LEADER... JUST DO IT....

Dick Bowman as Department Commander for the State of Arizona, Veterans of Foreign Wars, in 1935.

Dick was very active in the work of the Veterans of Foreign Wars for many years assisting in the installation of many VFW posts throughout the State of Arizona. He was a national delegate of the organization for the state in the 1930's.

DRESSIN' A COWBOY IN FORMAL ATTIRE
IS LIKE PUTTIN' EARRINGS IN A PIG'S EAR

Dick Bowman, my father, at age 73, dressed as a preacher in the filming of the movie, <u>The</u> <u>Great</u> <u>White</u> <u>Hope</u>, in Globe, Arizona, in 1969.

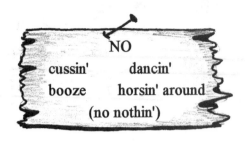

NO
cussin'   dancin'
booze   horsin' around
(no nothin')

PLEASE REMOVE
yer hat
yer spurs

TODAY'S SERMON
(a multitude of topics)

A CLOSED MOUTH CATCHETH NO FOOT...

BE CAREFUL WHAT YA DO WITH WHAT YA GOT...

**LIVE EVERYDAY LIKE IT WAS YER LAST,
CAUSE SOMEDAY YOU'LL BE RIGHT....**

Kids

YOUTH IS SUCH A WONDERFUL THING...
IT'S A SHAME TO WASTE IT ON KIDS

WHEN YOU'RE ON THE JOB, JUST KEEP
BURNIN' YER ROPE

Our older son
David G. Bowman, M.D. at age one and one-half.

Had a helluva start here on a fourth-generation Arizona Bowman cowman, but he jumped the *TRACES* and became a Specialist in Internal Medicine from the College of Medicine, University of Arizona at Tucson, Arizona.

He currently works in private practice, associated with St. Mary's Hospital in Tucson, Arizona.

ANTICIPATION IS GREATER THAN REALIZATION

Dr. David Bowman, age one and one-half, at Steve Bixby's
O Cross Ranch, at Globe, Arizona, in 1951.

**RIDIN' BULLS STILL REQUIRES THE SAME
PROCEDURE AS ALWAYS... A LEG ON EACH
SIDE AND THE MIND IN THE MIDDLE... IT'S THE
MIND THAT STILL SEEMS TO KEEP CAUSING
THE TROUBLE....**

A *STOMP ASS* **COWBOY NEEDS TENDER LOVIN' CARE....**

Our younger son
Douglas E. Bowman

Had another good start here on a fourth-generation Arizona Bowman cowman, but he too went astray. Doug studied Special Education at the University of Arizona at Tucson, Arizona, and is currently Prinicipal of Howenstine High School, a public school for the handicapped.

THE DOG WOULDA' CAUGHT THE
RABBIT IF HE HADN'T STOPPED
TO TAKE A
LEAK....

SOMETIMES YA JUST
GOTTA GO WITH THE
FLOW....

Ranchin'

YER ROPE WON'T GET RUSTY HANGIN' FROM YER SADDLE HORN

At six months, I got a fair start in the ranchin' business, 1924.

WHEN YER ALL *SCATTER-ASSED*, YER HORSE IS TOO

WHEN YA *DINK* A HORSE THAT'S *HARD ON GRAIN*, YOUR'RE DAMN SURE AFOOT

YOU'LL NEVER GET A DIPLOMA FROM THE *SCHOOL OF HARD KNOCKS....***BUT** **YOU'LL SURE AS HELL REMEMBER ITS LESSONS**

Classroom for the *SCHOOL OF HARD KNOCKS*

The Hook and Line Ranch headquarters in 1914, at the confluence of the Gila River and Hawk Canyon, six miles below Coolidge Dam, Arizona.

Ed Bowman, at age 33, managed the Hook and Line Ranch for this father-in-law, George Graham in 1919. This was nine years before the completion of Coolidge Dam, some six miles upstream on the Gila River. There were no roads so every item needed for man and ranch had to be *PACKED* in by mule over incredible terrain. Rupkey's store at Old San Carlos on the San Carlos Indian Reservation, some fifteen miles upstream on the Gila, was the closest place for supplies. At best, the *PACK* trip over the mule trail was not for the weak hearted. In flood stage, the river trip was next to an unbelieveable experience for the average cowboy. (Ed Bowman and George Graham certainly weren't average!)

Over the years, more than one pack mule and saddle horse were accidently drowned in the river. "But," Uncle Ed elated, "We never lost a man, although it was close a couple of times! One time I roped a cowboy right around the neck and pulled him out of the river. He had panicked while horseback in the swift swimming water and bailed off his horse. The guy didn't know how to swim and luckily his head kept bobbing up and down like a cork. His head was the only target I had to throw my rope at, so in one of his 'bobb ups,' I laced it on him. That was the maddest feller ya ever saw after I got him out because the rope burned his neck and he said I choked the liver out of him!"

Uncle Ed ultimately homesteaded at the Hook and Line and with the "stayin' power of a cockroach," he improved the economic cattle ranching unit. He built a road,* fences, cattle watering facilities and a fine home.

* The road, built by hand and with draft mule teams by Uncle Ed and his cowboys over horrendous terrain, circumvented the river. It never was much to brag about, as anyone who ever traversed it could testify. However, it sure beat the hell out of the *PACK* mule trail!

Coolidge Dam on U.S. Highway 70 between Safford and Globe, Arizona

The Hook and Line Ranch north fence line. Sure didn't have to worry about fixin' that *WATER GAP!*

**DON'T JUMP OFF A BLUFF TILL YA KNOW
HOW HIGH IT IS**

IT'S A GOOD IDEA TO KNOW WHICH WAY IS UP

BEFORE

AND AFTER

Top picture is Louise Bowman, wife of Ed on her way to the Hook and Line Ranch in 1919, six miles down stream on the Gila River. She is at the exact site where the proposed Coolidge Dam was later constructed.

Bottom picture is the completed dam, sometime after its dedication in 1928.

YA CAN'T COOK WITH COLD GREASE

George Graham's, Hook and Line chuck wagon in 1919. Never did figger out how the hell he got it there or if he ever moved it around once it was parked. The only place you could use a wheel on that outfit was about five miles up Hawk Canyon, and maybe a couple of miles up the Gila River at low water time.

LIFE IS PLAIN AND SIMPLE... THERE AIN'T NO FREE LUNCH....

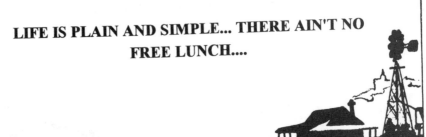

TREAT A MAD RATTLESNAKE AND A CHUCK WAGON COOK ALIKE... DON'T MESS WITH EITHER ONE....

WHEN A COWBOY STARTS WEARING SUSPENDERS, YOU CAN BET HE HAS CHECKED IN WITH HIS SOCIAL SECURITY REP. AND HE PROBABLY HAS A JOB COOKIN'

SOME BANKER'S COMPASSION IS NO BIGGER'N A BAR OF SOAP AFTER A MONDAY'S WASH

Louise Bowman, wife of Ed, in 1920 and her
Hook and Line, "Laundromat."

A COWMAN REALLY SHOULD GIVE HIS WIFE AS MUCH ATTENTION AS HE GIVES HIS COWS

THE GLORY IN THE COW BUSINESS IS MOSTLY SIZZLE AND LITTLE STEAK....

Granny's recipe for the wash

By John Van Deusen

What sort of advice could a bride expect from her grandmother back in 1800?

At least one woman saw fit to tell her granddaughter how to handle the family washing. This is an authentic recipe in its original spelling:

1. bild a fire in back yard to heet kettle of rain water
2. set tubs so smoke won't blow in eyes if wind is pert
3. shave 1 hole cake soap in bilin water
4. sort things—make 2 piles, 1 pile white, 1 pile cullord
5. stur flour in cold water, to smooth, then thin down with bilin water
6. rub dirty spots on board, scrub hard, then bile, rub cullord but dont bile—just rench
7. take white things out of kettle with broom stick handle, then rench, blew, and starch
8. spred tee towels on grass
9. hang old rags on fence
10. pore rench water in flower bed
11. scrub porch with hot soapy water
12. turn tubs upside down
13. go put on cleen dress—smooth hair with side combs—brew cup of tee—set and rest and rock a spell and count blessings.

A COWMAN HAS A LOVE FOR HIS RANGELAND AS INTENSE AS HIS LOVE FOR HIS CATTLE. HE WILL FIGHT LIKE HELL FOR BOTH

The scene at the Hook and Line Ranch headquarters changed from the time W.O. Tuttle originally established the ranch in 1898. A new house and three acres of cleared land in front helped considerably.

The ground was cleared of dense mesquite trees by Uncle Everett to develop a practice roping arena. He hooked a two mule team to the trees at slightly above ground level and hollered, "Get up." While the team strained on their *TRACES,* he chopped on the tree with an axe on the opposite side where he had dug down below the crown of the tree's roots. The wise mules fell on their faces only once; just the first time when the tree broke loose!

IT'S HARD TO RIDE A *BRONC* WHEN YER SADDLE'S SITTIN' *WHOPPER JAWED*

Spring Roundup

Ed Bowman, John Ortega, Leon Bowman, Ed's son, and I, rounding up on the Hook and Line Ranch in 1947.

RIDIN' ANOTHER MAN'S SADDLE IS LIKE TRYIN' TO WEAR HIS BOOTS

A COWBOY CAN REMEMBER MULTITUDES OF COWS... TOO BAD HE'S NOT AS GOOD WITH PEOPLE'S NAMES....

WHEN YA GET RIGHT OUT TO THE EDGE OF THE EARTH, IT MIGHT PAY TO TAKE A LOOK BACK

Barbara Butler Bowman

My wife soon after our marriage in 1948, at the "Edge of the Earth" on the Hook and Line Ranch at the confluence of Hawk Canyon and the Gila River, six miles below Coolidge Dam, Arizona.

Before our marriage, Barbara worked for the Penn Mutual Life Insurance Co. in Phoenix. In 1964, while continuing to pursue my goals as a cattleman, I accepted an additional challenge with the New York Life Insurance Company as a Field Underwriter, Barbara's only reply to this revolutionary decision was, "My heavens, I could have married a life insurance peddler twenty years ago!"

JUST KEEP SPURRIN', SOONER OR LATER YOU'LL FIND A WAY OFF A ONE-WAY ROAD

The bridge over the Gila River, one mile from the Hook
and Line Ranch house, in 1949.

Barbara, my wife, could drive like a pro over the eight
miles of rough, narrow road to Coolidge Dam (it took forty
minutes,) but she balked at the bridge; that's Barbara afoot.

RANCHIN' IS HELL ON HORSES
AND WOMEN

NOT EVERYTHING IN THE COW BUSINESS IS "HEAD DOWN AND ASS UP"; A LOT OF IT IS "ASS UP AND HEAD DOWN"

Branding time at the Hook and Line ranch in 1948.
That's Ed in the appropriate position of the cow business.

PUTTIN' YOURSELF IN THE OTHER FELLER'S BOOTS CAN TURN ON A LOT OF LIGHTS....

DON'T WORRY ABOUT THE BUCKLES OF YOUR
SPURS **BEING ON THE INSIDE OR THE OUTSIDE**
OF YOUR INSTEP... THE IMPORTANT THING IS
THE SHARPNESS OF YOUR *ROWELS*....

Spring branding time at the Hook and Line. Hope Ed didn't
rear back real quick!

WHEN YA GOT A WILD COW
YOKED TO A SAPLIN'....
YA GOT 'ER CONTAINED....

DON'T LOOK BACK MUCH UNLESS YOU ARE
RIDIN' IN THE LEAD OF THE HERD

The Hook and Line trail herd on the two day drive from Coolidge Dam, Arizona, to the railroad shipping pens at San Carlos, Arizona, in the spring of 1950.

YA GOTTA HAVE A GAME PLAN BEFORE YA
CAN START A CATTLE DRIVE

A COWBOY HAS TO HAVE THE ABILITY TO
FLY BY THE SEAT OF HIS PANTS

The author and his plane at the Hook and Line Ranch in 1948. The Aeronica sure beat the hell out of a pack mule for puttin' block salt out for the cattle and it was a lot more fun.

JOANIE SAYS THAT COWS ARE GOOD, BUT
ONCE IN AWHILE A COWMAN HAS TO
HAVE A NEW LITTLE RED WAGON

**IN A CATTLE TRADE, BE SURE YOU DON'T
GET YOUR ASS OUT IN FRONT OF
YOUR POCKET BOOK**

Louise and Lewis Bowman weighing the sale cattle at
the Hook and Line Ranch in 1948.

CAVEAT EMPTOR **SURE ENOUGH APPLIES
TO CATTLE BUYING**

**IF YA GET *SCOOPED* IN A COW TRADE,
BE SURE YA KNOW WHAT
CAUSED IT**

TO THE COWBOY, THE DIFFERENCE BETWEEN A GOOD MEAL AND A BAD ONE IS THE LENGTH OF TIME BETWEEN THEM

In 1922, my uncles Everett and Skeet Bowman, at ages twenty-three and twenty, along with eight other cowboys, drove a sizable herd of cattle from Globe, Arizona, to Ely, Nevada, for the JK ranch. Their exact route is not known now, but this cattle drive consumed the bigger part of the summer. Needless to say, they encountered many difficulties along the nine hundred mile trip; the worst being that they almost lost their chuckwagon at the crossing of the Colorado River. I'll bet Metro Goldwyn Mayer wished they had been along.

IF YOU ARE CONTINUALLY LOOKIN'
FOR A *BUGGER*, YER APT TO
FIND ONE....

IF YER GONNA KILL TIME, WORK IT TO DEATH

Everett Bowman squatted down reading, with the JK
wagon near Ely, Nevada, in 1922.

IF EVERYONE IS DOIN' THE SAME THING, NO
ONE IS DOIN' ANYTHING

EVERY DAY IS "EARTH DAY"
FOR A COWMAN

My uncles, Everett and Skeet Bowman then young cowboys in 1922, went from Globe, Arizona, to Ely, Nevada, on a nine hundred mile cattle drive. Having grown up in the rough, rocky range lands around Safford, Arizona, their plan was to make the flat, easy terrain of Nevada their future in the cowpunchin' business. However, one cold severe winter in the "North Land," *SET THE HAIR* on the southern Arizona cowboys and they decided to go home and try their luck at the rodeo game. There was no bus or rail transportation available and they didn't have a car for the one thousand mile trip. So they pulled out on their two horses, the only thing they owned.

They made it in a little over a month's time, where upon Everett reported, "We would have made it a helluva lot sooner but every time we came across a cow track full of water, Skeet had to stop and wash his damn clothes!"

YA NEVER HAVE TO JUMP-START A GOOD COWBOY... HE'S WOUND UP ALL THE TIME

THE AMOUNT OF HARD WORK THAT A
COWBOY CAN TAKE DEPENDS ON
HOW HE IS GEARED

Everett Bowman, a JK cowboy at Ely, Nevada, in 1922.

**THE MOST IMPORTANT
OBJECTIVE IN SHOEIN'
A HORSE IS TO GET
THE SUCKER ON IRON**

SHOEIN' **HORSES CAN
MAKE YA WISH YOU'DA
TOOK UP SCHOOL
TEACHIN'**

STAY AWAY FROM THOSE SWINGIN' DOORS
AND TELL 'EM YOU'RE A VIRGO

Skeet Bowman at Ely, Nevada, in 1924.

Uncle Skeet and his brother Everett, punched cows for the JK's near Ely for about a year. Being raised in rough, southern Arizona country, the flat lands and cold winters "didn't take" on them. They went home and launched rodeo careers which proved successful for both of them.

A FELLER'S NOT AT TOP PERFORMANCE WHEN
HE IS OLD ENOUGH TO KNOW BETTER, BUT
TOO YOUNG TO CARE

THEY IMPROVED IT... HOMESTEADED IT...
TOOK CARE OF IT....

Everett and Skeet Bowman building the road to their
A Dart Ranch, west of Safford, Arizona, in the early 1930's.

My uncles didn't have much to work with when they
bought their ranch at Stanley Butte, west of Safford, but
they certainly weren't short on desire. They borrowed this
"modern" road building equipment and with the determination of a tumblebug, carved a productive cow and horse
ranch out of this hostile, rugged country.

TODAY IS THE FIRST DAY OF THE REST OF YOUR LIFE

H. Skeet Bowman, Sheriff of Graham County,
Safford, Arizona.

In 1940, Uncle Skeet went to work as a deputy for Graham County Sheriff, Vick Christensen in Safford, Arizona, while continuing to operate his ranch at Stanley Butte. At the end of Vick's two terms in office, Skeet was elected sheriff. He held that position for twenty- two years. This broke a precedent among voters that allowed a sheriff to serve only two, two-year terms.

THE PROCESS OF *SHOEIN'* A HORSE IS ABOUT AS SLICK AS A WET *LATTIGO*

WHEN YA GOT A TOUGH JOB TO DO.... DON'T HOLD BACK

ANY JOB OUTSIDE IS A HELLUVA LOT BETTER THAN ONE IN THE HOUSE

THE WORST PART OF A JOB IS JUST GETTIN' TO IT

YOU CAN TELL A LOT ABOUT A COWMAN BY JUST LOOKIN' AT HIS COWS

Ed Bowman on the right, and some of his registered
Hereford herd near Peyton, Colorado in 1950.

Uncle Ed maintained a breeding unit of quality Herefords
at his Payton ranch for the purpose of supplying replace-
ment bulls for his Arizona ranch. He selected his best-raised
bulls at weaning time in the fall of the year and took them to
Arizona for further development. The results of his
procedure considerably up-graded the quality of his Arizona
cattle.

THE WORST TROUBLE WITH LOAFING IS YOU NEVER KNOW WHEN YOU'RE DONE

Home base of the famous Lee Brothers at Blue, Arizona, about 1940. The five brothers were ranchers and internationally known professional hunters. A couple of them are shown here, along with a couple of hunting clients and Ed Bowman in the doorway. The experiences of the Lees throughout the United States, Mexico, and several other foreign countries would fill a volume; wish someone would write it if it hasn't been done to date.

EVERYBODY NEEDS A TRAFFIC COP DOC

David G. Bowman, M.D., Tucson, Arizona, my older son. While his medical career is his true love, David hasn't forgotten his cow ranch roots. He still helps me at the ranch occasionally whenever he can get a day or two away from his patients.

GOOD THINGS COME TO THOSE WHO WORK
LIKE HELL

TIME FOR REJOICING IS WHEN THE
CATTLE ARE SHIPPED

Fall shipping on the IGO Ranch at the base of the
Chiricahua Mountains.

Larry Moore and Roger Riggs, Arizona cattle ranchers,
helping their neighbor, Tom Kuykendall.

WHEN A COWMAN THROWS A PARTY, HE
USUALLY OPENS A *KEG OF NAILS*

WHEN ASKED WHAT HIS CATTLE
BROUGHT ON THE MARKET...
THE COWMAN REPLIED,
"TEARS TO MY EYES"

The life of the cattleman and cowboy is filled with sun, storm and mist... The same as any other human being's.

The difference lies in an intense love for a way of life, a complex feeling, that can be no easier conveyed on a piece of paper than the wind that sighs across the sand or soft cloud shadows on the mountains.

YA HAVE TO LIVE IT

TO FEEL IT....

Rodeo

Everett Bowman of Wickenburg, Arizona, known by many of his contemporaries as "The Cowboy's Cowboy."

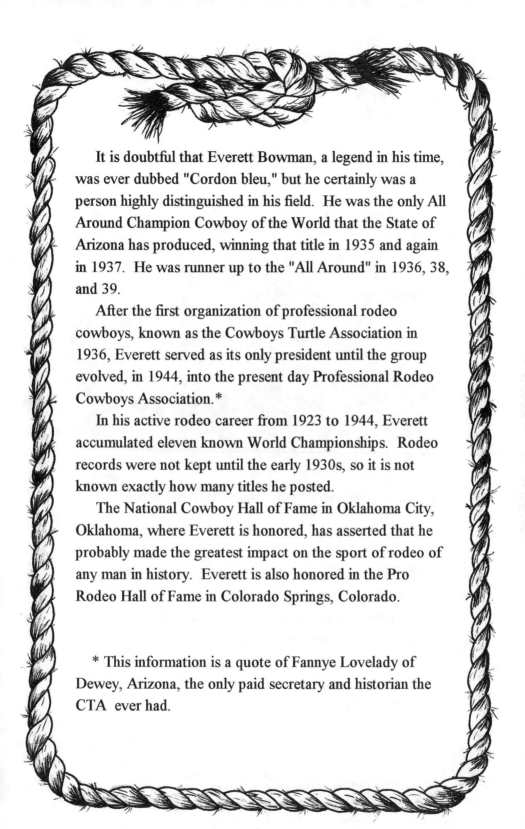

It is doubtful that Everett Bowman, a legend in his time, was ever dubbed "Cordon bleu," but he certainly was a person highly distinguished in his field. He was the only All Around Champion Cowboy of the World that the State of Arizona has produced, winning that title in 1935 and again in 1937. He was runner up to the "All Around" in 1936, 38, and 39.

After the first organization of professional rodeo cowboys, known as the Cowboys Turtle Association in 1936, Everett served as its only president until the group evolved, in 1944, into the present day Professional Rodeo Cowboys Association.*

In his active rodeo career from 1923 to 1944, Everett accumulated eleven known World Championships. Rodeo records were not kept until the early 1930s, so it is not known exactly how many titles he posted.

The National Cowboy Hall of Fame in Oklahoma City, Oklahoma, where Everett is honored, has asserted that he probably made the greatest impact on the sport of rodeo of any man in history. Everett is also honored in the Pro Rodeo Hall of Fame in Colorado Springs, Colorado.

* This information is a quote of Fannye Lovelady of Dewey, Arizona, the only paid secretary and historian the CTA ever had.

NECESSITY IS THE MOTHER OF INVENTION

Ed Bowman, calf roping on "Pete" at Chicago in 1927.

While Everett Bowman has been described as the George Washington of professional rodeo, his older brother, Ed Bowman of Coolidge Dam, Arizona, could well be noted as the Thomas Jefferson.

It has been said by his peers that Ed was the man who "wrote the rule book" on pro roping. He brought many innovations to the pro rodeo arena, the most revolutionary

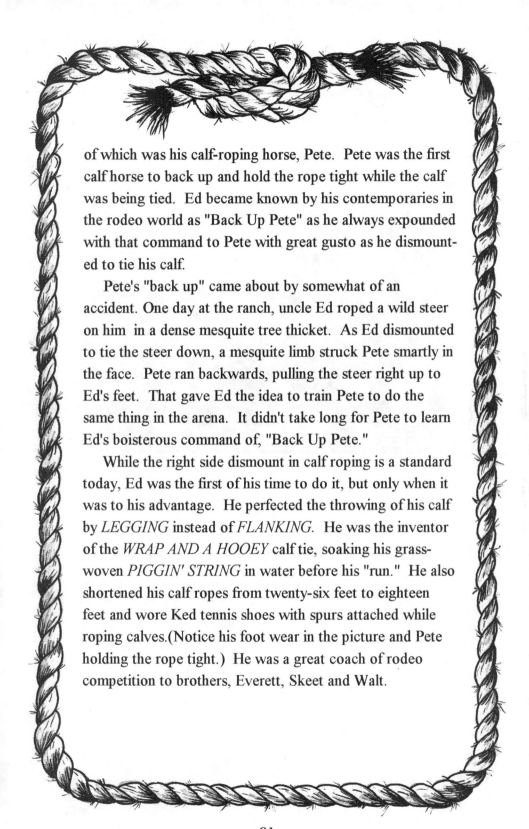

of which was his calf-roping horse, Pete. Pete was the first calf horse to back up and hold the rope tight while the calf was being tied. Ed became known by his contemporaries in the rodeo world as "Back Up Pete" as he always expounded with that command to Pete with great gusto as he dismounted to tie his calf.

Pete's "back up" came about by somewhat of an accident. One day at the ranch, uncle Ed roped a wild steer on him in a dense mesquite tree thicket. As Ed dismounted to tie the steer down, a mesquite limb struck Pete smartly in the face. Pete ran backwards, pulling the steer right up to Ed's feet. That gave Ed the idea to train Pete to do the same thing in the arena. It didn't take long for Pete to learn Ed's boisterous command of, "Back Up Pete."

While the right side dismount in calf roping is a standard today, Ed was the first of his time to do it, but only when it was to his advantage. He perfected the throwing of his calf by *LEGGING* instead of *FLANKING*. He was the inventor of the *WRAP AND A HOOEY* calf tie, soaking his grass-woven *PIGGIN' STRING* in water before his "run." He also shortened his calf ropes from twenty-six feet to eighteen feet and wore Ked tennis shoes with spurs attached while roping calves.(Notice his foot wear in the picture and Pete holding the rope tight.) He was a great coach of rodeo competition to brothers, Everett, Skeet and Walt.

CHEYENNE OR BUST

Brothers Everett, at age 27, and Skeet Bowman, age 24, in the early days of their rodeo careers. They were enroute from Safford, Arizona to the Cheyenne Frontier Days Rodeo in 1926. Their horse trailer, the first ever seen on the rodeo circuit, was made by their older brother, Dick, in a matter of a few hours. It took them the better part of a week to make this trip of some 1,000 miles; roads weren't top notch in those days, nor was their equipment. They were either stopping to patch a tire or looking for a stream to park in, to soak the wooden spokes of their wheels.

A COWBOY IS LIKE A CHICKEN HAWK, HE DOESN'T MISS A THING

Arizona cowboys, Jack Trainor and Everett Bowman on the rodeo trail in 1926.

It's hard to imagine how the rodeo contestants of this era were able to attend enough "shows" to make a living. Many of them didn't, but a few like Uncle Everett somehow prevailed at this sport as a full time successful occupation. Everett said, "Getting around fast enough was our biggest problem and travel was expensive. We lived in a tent and cooked our own meals but fixed costs were high. Gasoline alone for the eleven month tour in 1935 was a whooping twelve hundred dollars!"

"WONDER WHERE I PUT MY TOOTH BRUSH?"

Skeet Bowman of Safford, Arizona, with brother Everett, in their Dodge pickup and Bowman trailer on the pro rodeo circuit at Gallup, New Mexico, in 1927. Of the four Bowman brothers who competed in the earlier days of rodeo, Skeet was without question the best roper. He won several *RAA* calf ropings, and was hailed by his peers as one of the best team roping headers of his time.

After Everett and he made a stake in rodeo by the early 1930's, they made a down payment on a cow ranch near Stanley Butte, west of Safford, Arizona. Skeet operated the ranch and started raising children (six of them), rodeoing more sparingly from then on. He ultimately acquired the ranch for his sole ownership, and Everett bought another one for his personal account near Hillside, Arizona.

**IT'S HARD TO GET ANYTHING DONE WHEN
EVERYTHING IS *OUT OF KILTER***

Skeet and Lois Bowman rollin' up their "Roadside Inn"
at Wickenberg, Arizona, on the 1927 rodeo trail.

CHOMPIN' AT THE BIT **CAN GET YER CYLINDER
HEAD TEMPERATURE UP**

**TIME WAITS FOR NO ONE, USE HELL OUT
OF IT WHILE YA GOT IT**

FEATHERED OUT IN GLAD RAGS

Everett and Skeet Bowman *DUDED UP* on the rodeo trail with their famous Bowman horse trailer between Superior and Miami, Arizona, in 1927.

The three Bowman brothers and most of the rodeo cowboys usually wore their best clothes when out in public. Carl Arnold, Jake McClure, Manerd Gayler, Richard Merchant, Hugh Bennett, C.B. Irwin, Doc Pardee, to name a few of the top *HANDS,* were noted for often wearing neckties when appearing in the rodeo arena. Time changes everything!

IT'S A WEALTHY MAN WHO ENJOYS HIS WORK EACH DAY

Skeet and Everett Bowman on the rodeo trail in their Dodge truck in 1927. Can you imagine three people riding in the cab of this thing for thousands of miles over those kinds of roads, eleven months out of the year? Aunt Lois, Everett's wife doubled as the tour photographer. These people really had to love their work!

IF YOU JERK ON YOUR OWN BOOT STRAPS ENOUGH, SOMETHING WILL FINALLY HAPPEN

The Bowman brothers, Skeet, Everett and Ed in their "motel" at the Warren Ball Park, Bisbee, Arizona Rodeo, in 1927. The three brothers often traveled together on the rodeo circuit and "partnered" together in their winnings. Ed made a bet with his neighboring rancher in the Globe, Arizona, area that at least one of the three of them would win something at every rodeo they participated in during the full year of their competition. The bet was for a hundred dollar Stetson hat, and they had to participate in at least thirty rodeos. Ed looked mighty good in his new hat at the end of the year! (A hat of comparable quality today cost in excess of fifteen hundred dollars.)

Pioneers of private air travel on the rodeo circuit in 1929.

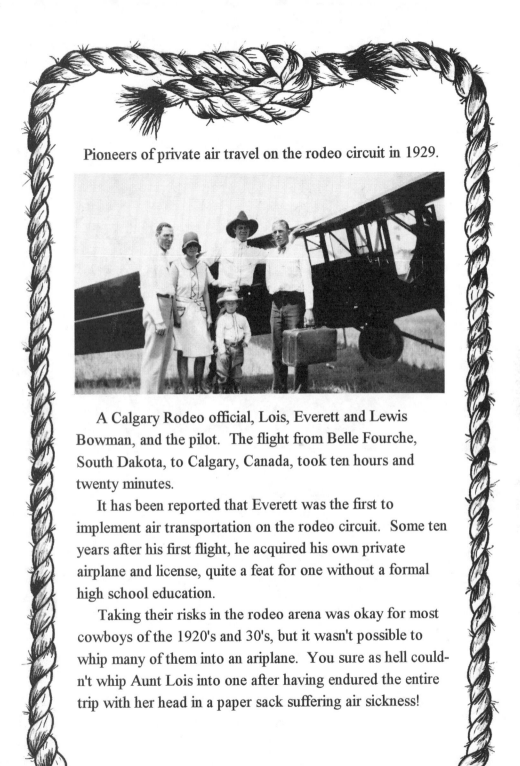

A Calgary Rodeo official, Lois, Everett and Lewis Bowman, and the pilot. The flight from Belle Fourche, South Dakota, to Calgary, Canada, took ten hours and twenty minutes.

It has been reported that Everett was the first to implement air transportation on the rodeo circuit. Some ten years after his first flight, he acquired his own private airplane and license, quite a feat for one without a formal high school education.

Taking their risks in the rodeo arena was okay for most cowboys of the 1920's and 30's, but it wasn't possible to whip many of them into an ariplane. You sure as hell couldn't whip Aunt Lois into one after having endured the entire trip with her head in a paper sack suffering air sickness!

"NO PROBLEM FELLERS!"

(UH - HUH... AND IF AUNT MINNIE HAD BALLS
SHE'D BE YOUR UNCLE)

WHEN YA GOT A SPARKPLUG IN YER OUTFIT, LET 'IM FIRE, BUT BE SURE YER DISTRIBUTOR STAYS HOOKED UP

Uncle Everett and me at the launching of Junior Rodeo in Dallas, Texas, in 1929.

Our white shirts were made by Susan Bowman, Everett's mother and my grandmother, from the heavy cloth sacks that packaged ninety-six pounds of cement. Everett was somewhat of a superstitious person; he was wearing one of these shirts at the time of one of his early day rodeo wins, so for years thereafter, he would wear nothing but a white shirt while competing in his rodeo events.

**RUNNIN' A COW OUTFIT
IS LIKE DANCIN' WITH A
BEAR; YOU'RE NOT DONE
'TILL THE BEAR IS**

Lewis and a bear at the Chicago,
Illinois, rodeo in conjunction with
the Worlds Fair, in 1933.

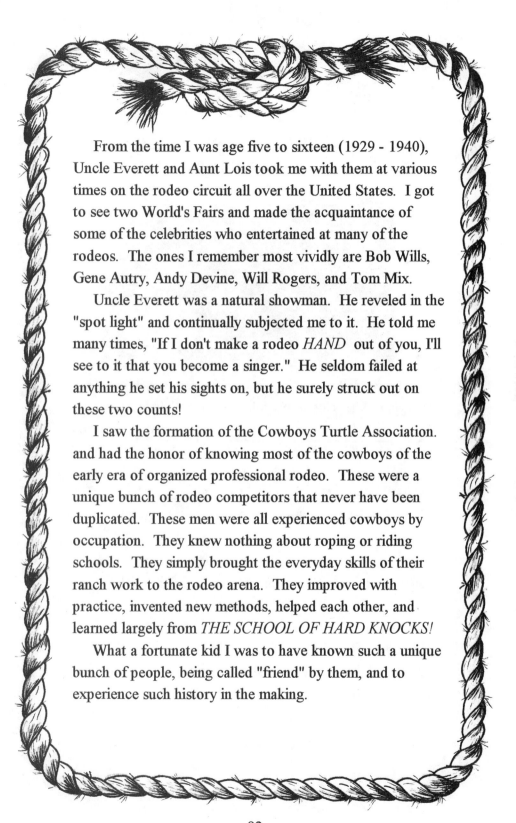

From the time I was age five to sixteen (1929 - 1940), Uncle Everett and Aunt Lois took me with them at various times on the rodeo circuit all over the United States. I got to see two World's Fairs and made the acquaintance of some of the celebrities who entertained at many of the rodeos. The ones I remember most vividly are Bob Wills, Gene Autry, Andy Devine, Will Rogers, and Tom Mix.

Uncle Everett was a natural showman. He reveled in the "spot light" and continually subjected me to it. He told me many times, "If I don't make a rodeo *HAND* out of you, I'll see to it that you become a singer." He seldom failed at anything he set his sights on, but he surely struck out on these two counts!

I saw the formation of the Cowboys Turtle Association. and had the honor of knowing most of the cowboys of the early era of organized professional rodeo. These were a unique bunch of rodeo competitors that never have been duplicated. These men were all experienced cowboys by occupation. They knew nothing about roping or riding schools. They simply brought the everyday skills of their ranch work to the rodeo arena. They improved with practice, invented new methods, helped each other, and learned largely from *THE SCHOOL OF HARD KNOCKS!*

What a fortunate kid I was to have known such a unique bunch of people, being called "friend" by them, and to experience such history in the making.

WHEN YA KNOW YOU'VE DONE A GOOD JOB, YA FEEL AS BIG AS A HOOP ON A BARREL

Everybody had a job on the rodeo "run", including the five-year olds. One of my jobs was to gather firewood or cowchips, whatever was available, for our tent campground.

COOLING OUT the horses after they had been used by the cowboys, was my main duty. I "cooled" horses for Uncle Everett, Hugh Bennett, Erby Munday, Richard Merchant, Jake McClure, Ike Rude, Carl Arnold, Earl Thode, John McEntire, and many other cowboys. I really took to this job, cause I liked to ride, and got paid well. I usually got a quarter, sometimes half a dollar for thirty to forty minutes of my time. Carl Arnold once gave me a silver dollar, the first one I ever had. I can remember how I felt.. kinda like I had my fortune made! I still have that teasured dollar in my possession after sixty-five years. I wouldn't part with that dollar for anything.

**THERE'S PLENTY OF HORSES THAT CAN TURN
YA** *ASS OVER TEA CUP*

Frank Van Meter takin' a *DIVE ASS* at Livingston,
Montana, in the 1930's.

**NEVER LET YOUR EGO WRITE CHECKS YER
BODY ISN'T ABLE TO CASH**

DAMN SHAME THE WORLD AIN'T LEVEL

A GOOD GUIDE TO THE STATE OF ECONOMY OF THE CATTLE BUSINESS IS TO TAKE NOTE OF THE AGE AND CONDITION OF THE VEHICLES AROUND A LIVESTOCK OPERATION

Skeet Bowman roping at Round Valley, Arizona.
Note the rodeo arena construction in the early 1930's.

A MAN HAS A LOT OF *BOTTOM* WHEN HE HANDLES HIS TROUBLES WITHOUT COMPLAININ'

WHEN YOU'RE *TRAILIN'* DEEP TRACKS AND THIN MANURE, YA SURE BETTER FIND OUT WHAT THE HELL CAUSED 'EM

Pancho Villa Jr., bull fighting in the early 1930's.

Don't know what the bull's name was but I think Pancho had a special moniker for him! Pancho let this bull hit him at least once during each performance of the show. He knew the bull real well, and the bull knew Pancho, but it still took one helluva athlete to pull this act off repeatedly without serious consequences.

WHEN YA DO THINGS RIGHT... THE REST JUST FOLLOWS....

Everett Bowman, calf roping on Chino in 1931.

Uncle Everett won the Calf Roping World Championship in 1929, 1935, 1937; all of them from thirty to sixty foot *SCORES*. He won the Steer Roping World Championship from the same length *SCORES* in 1937. The steers weighed a thousand pounds or more; the roping calves weighed four hundred pounds or more.

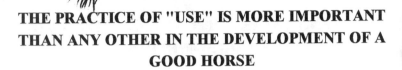

THE PRACTICE OF "USE" IS MORE IMPORTANT THAN ANY OTHER IN THE DEVELOPMENT OF A GOOD HORSE

Everett Bowman loading Chino at Yellowstone, Wyoming in 1934. Wow! Haven't horse trailers come a long way in ten years? It's too bad that brother Dick wasn't able to keep on with trailer manufacturing from the time he built the first one known to the rodeo world in 1924.

WHEN YOU'VE GOT PERSISTENCE AND DETERMINATION, YER *APT* TO GET SOMETHIN' DONE

WHEN YA WAKE UP, GET UP... WHEN YA GET UP, DO SOMETHING....

The "Holiday Inn" of Pro Rodeo in 1935.

Lois Bowman, wife of Everett doin' her camp chores at Madrone, California. Many a hungry cowboy frequented the Bowman's camp through the years, none were ever turned away.

IT SURE IS HARD TO FIND GOOD HELP WHEN YA GOT A TOUGH JOB

A GOOD WIFE COACHES HER MAN BEHIND THEIR BEDROOM DOOR

IF YA DON'T HAVE THE DESIRE TO COMPETE....
YA PROBABLY DON'T HAVE THE DESIRE TO
SUCCEED

Walt Bowman of Irvine, California, winning the bull-dogging at Prescott, Arizona, in 1925. Walt spent most of his lifetime working on cattle ranches in California, and participated in rodeo competition rarely; when he did, he was usually in the money.

GOOD POKER PLAYERS
DON'T BLINK

USUALLY YA CAN'T GET A CIGARETTE PAPER
BETWEEN FIRST AND SECOND PLACE

Ed Bowman winning the *STRAP AND CINCH RELAY RACE* at Prescott, Arizona in 1925. Ed retired undefeated in this special event after competing in it for nine years. His famous calf roping horse,"Back-Up Pete," was always his anchor mount in this race that required four different horses. The rider had to change his saddle to a new horse at a "station" each quarter of a mile through the course of the mile race around an oval race track. Too bad this rodeo event has not been continued; it was a thriller!

TAKIN' THE BULL BY THE HORNS IS ONE THING, MAKIN' SOMETHIN' OUT OF IT IS SOMETHIN' ELSE

The bulldogging steers at Calgary, Canada, in 1926 were so big (thirteen hundred pounds plus), the cowboys couldn't throw them on the first day of the "show", so the rodeo officials changed the contest to Steer Decorating.

Ed Bowman, at one hundred sixty pounds, won the event because he developed a way to slip the decorative red ribbon, attached to a rubber band, over the steer's left horn without trying to bring the huge animal to a stop. He practiced his decorating on a brass bed post most of the night before the contest, subsituting the rubber band with one of his wife's garters, as her leg wasn't much bigger than the steer's horn.

Everett Bowman bulldogging at Phoenix, Arizona, in 1940.

Here he was referred to as the "Human Gorilla." This steer weighed in excess of one thousand pounds. It was not uncommon in those days for the "doggin" steers to weigh as much as twelve hundred pounds and they were run from a fifteen to thirty foot *SCORE!* The *SCORE* was subsequently shortened to just a few feet, as they are today, and the weight of the steers has drastically been reduced.

WHEN YER ON TOP OF THE HEAP,
DON'T FORGET HOW YOU GOT THERE

Everett Bowman's "ALL AROUND" trophy buckle awarded by the Rodeo Association of America and was sponsored by Levi. Everett won two of these, one in 1935 and another 1937. They are on display at the Cowboy Hall of Fame, Oklahoma City, Oklahoma. Uncle Everett donated all of the trophies that he won (a whole station wagon load) in his twenty years of professional rodeo competition to the Cowboy Hall of Fame.

WHEN YA TAKE THE BULL BY THE HORNS, BE SURE YA HAVE YOUR FEET ON THE GROUND

Hugh Bennett, 6' 3", at two hundred thirty-five pounds, bulldogging his eleven hundred pound steer from a thirty foot *SCORE*, at Miles City, Montana, in 1936. Hugh said,"It sure was a good thing there was a back end to the arena or I might never have stopped this steer". His time was ninety-one seconds.

**IF YER GONNA DRIVE THE WAGON... BE SURE
TACT AND DIPLOMACY GO WITH YA....**

The 1927 Cheyenne Frontier Days parade in C. B. Irwin's "Hay Day". C. B., another of the "Old Timers" who had a decided effect on professional rodeo, is honored in the National Cowboy Hall of Fame in Oklahoma City.

**SOME THINGS JUMP WHEN YA CRACK THE
WHIP... BUT NOT ALL OF THEM**

AMBITION IS THE TRIGGER TO
ACCOMPLISHMENT

    C.B. Irwin's rodeo headquarters on the circuit in the 1920's. The large feller in the middle is C.B.. He was one of the granddaddy's of the big early day rodeo producers and probably "The One" who made the Cheyenne Frontier Days. He hired many of the top *HANDS* by paying their way on his private railroad cars and entering them at the shows for a percentage of their winnings. His philosophy was, "If ya can't beat him, buy him." C.B. was an uncanny horsemen, breeding and training many successful race horses. He was also a champion steer roper in the 1920's.

GETTIN' OLD AIN'T FOR SISSIES

"Packsaddle" Ben Greenough, Red Lodge, Montana, father of eight Greenough bronc riders. Ben did the inlay work in his rifle with elk horn.

"THESE GOLDEN YEARS ARE THE SHITS"

Ɛ-Ɛ

Margie Greenough Henson and Alice Greenough Orr at the Tucson, Arizona Rodeo in 1980.

These sisters are honored in the National Cowgirl Hall of Fame in Hereford, Texas, the National Cowboy Hall of Fame in Oklahoma City, Oklahoma, and the Montana Sports Hall of Fame in Billings, Montana.

ARTISTIC IMPRESSION IS CREATED BY A GOOD BRONC RIDE

Margie Greenough Henson of Tucson, Arizona, at Sun Valley, Idaho, in the late 1930's. She is honored in the National Cowgirl Hall of Fame, Hereford, Texas; National Cowboy Hall of Fame, Oklahoma City, Oklahoma, and the Montana Sports Hall of Fame in Billings, Montana.

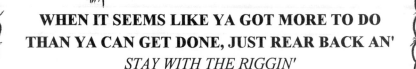

WHEN IT SEEMS LIKE YA GOT MORE TO DO THAN YA CAN GET DONE, JUST REAR BACK AN' *STAY WITH THE RIGGIN'*

Margie Greenough Henson making a *CLASSIC* ride at a Leo Cremer rodeo in the 1930's. Margie designed and made all of her riding clothes.

HANG 'EM IN 'IM

"Alice Greenough" "Riding a Bronc".

Alice Greenough making another *CLASSIC* ride at New Harmony, Indiana, in 1935.

**RUNNIN' A BUSINESS IS LIKE RIDIN' A BRONC...
YA BETTER *BE WITH HIM* THE FIRST JUMP
OUT OF THE CHUTE....**

BE SURE YA TAKE *WILLIE* WITH YA

Author's note: While *Bumfuzzled* was in press, we learned of the passing of another of the famous "history makers" of professional rodeo. Alice died in Tucson on August 20, 1995.

UNSURPASSED RODEO BEAUTY

Alice and Margie Greenough on their *QUADRILLE*
horses at a Leo Cremer rodeo in the mid 1930's.

If you've never seen a square dance performed on horseback, you've missed something! These girls added a special
touch of class to it.

FIGHTIN' A MAD BULL IS LIKE WRESTLIN' WITH A LOCOED OCTOPUS

Rodeo clown, Charlie "Chuck" Henson of Tucson, Arizona, son of "Heavy" and Margie Henson, "saving Larry Mahan's life" in the 1960's.

ᏟᎢ

The general public has never given the rodeo clown credit for the job he does in the arena. Many cowboys owe their life and limb to these incredible showmen. The bravery and athletic ability exhibited by "the clown" has turned potential disasters into belly-rollin' crowd pleasers. Our hats are off to these masters of their profession.

HOLD A TIGHT ASS **IN TOUGH SITUATIONS**

1905 - 1995

Turk Greenough winning at the Calgary Stampede on Hat Rack in 1940. Turk was a Triple Crown winner in three different years. The crown was awarded to the bronc riding champion at Calgary, Pendleton, and Cheyenne.

WHEN YA GET ALL *DOLLED UP*... BE SURE YA GOT A PLACE TO GO....

OWGIRLS AT TEX AUSTINS RODEO CHICAGO, 1926

The Rodeo Cowgirls at Chicago in 1926. Fox Hasting, a saddle bronc rider and bulldogger, is third from the right. Wish we knew the rest of the girls, but it's been too long ago. If you recognize any of them, would appreciate it if ya dropped us a line.

WHEN COURTIN' THE BELLE OF THE BALL, BE SURE YOU DON'T GET YOUR *SPURS* TANGLED UP WITH HERS....

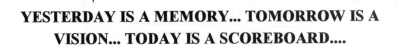

YESTERDAY IS A MEMORY... TOMORROW IS A VISION... TODAY IS A SCOREBOARD....

The winners at Prescott Frontier Days Rodeo in 1925. Ed and Everett Bowman are the first two mounted men on the left. (Ed's note: If ya can identify any of the others, please drop us a note.)

BELIEF IS PROBABLY AS IMPORTANT AS ABILITY

YOU'RE ONLY AS GOOD AS YER LAST ACCOMPLISHMENT

A Leo Cremer rodeo in Colorado in the mid 1930's.

The Colorado State Fair Queen, Colorado Governor Carr,
Leo Cremer, Paul Carney, and Everett Bowman.

Leo Cremer was a noted producer of many rodeos
throughout the nation. He was unbeatable in his acquisition
of exceptional bucking horses. Most of his real tough ones
came out of the Northern Mid-West States and Southern
Canada.

**YA GOT TO HAVE A COMPETITOR IN ORDER
TO EXCEL**

IT'S NOT AS FAR TO THE TOP OF THE STAIRS AS YA MIGHT THINK

Fay Blackstone, Margie Greenough, Nancy Sheppard, Dorothy Dollerhide, and Mary Iller at a Leo Cremer rodeo in Mandan, North Dakota, about 1935.

WHEN YA KEEP YER FACE TO THE SUN, THE SHADOWS ALWAYS FALL BEHIND YOU

Earl Thode of Belvidere, South Dakota, in 1927. The winner of the North American Championship at the Calgary, Canada Stampede. Earl was probably the man that paved the way to the keeping of rodeo records for the All Around Champion of the World. He no doubt would have achieved this title more than once had records been kept in the early days of his rodeo career. He was a top saddle bronc rider as well as a roper. He was the first man to be awarded the All Around title in 1929, the first year the *RAA* started the trend which has continued to the present time.

T+

**THERE ARE FEW PLACES WHERE YOU FIND
MORE HUMOR THAN ON A COW OUTFIT AND
FEWER PLACES WHERE YOU FIND MORE
SERIOUS PEOPLE**

Ralph Bennett, Ed Bowman, Hugh Bennett, and Skeet
Bowman at a matched team roping at the Broadmore in
Colorado Springs, Colorado, in 1949. The Bowmans barely
won on ten steers roped.

THERE'S NOTHING MORE POTENT THAN AN IDEA WHOSE TIME HAS COME

Bob Wills and his Texas Playboys in the 1930's.

Bob has been credited as the guy who created the popularity of western music. It's doubtful he had any idea that it would reach the magnitude it is today, even though the style is somewhat different now.

Bob was a real friend of rodeo and all the cowboys. Full of life and enthusiasm, he always drew top billing. This bunch of cowboys really liked to dance, so the show was considered a success when Bob and his Playboys were present.

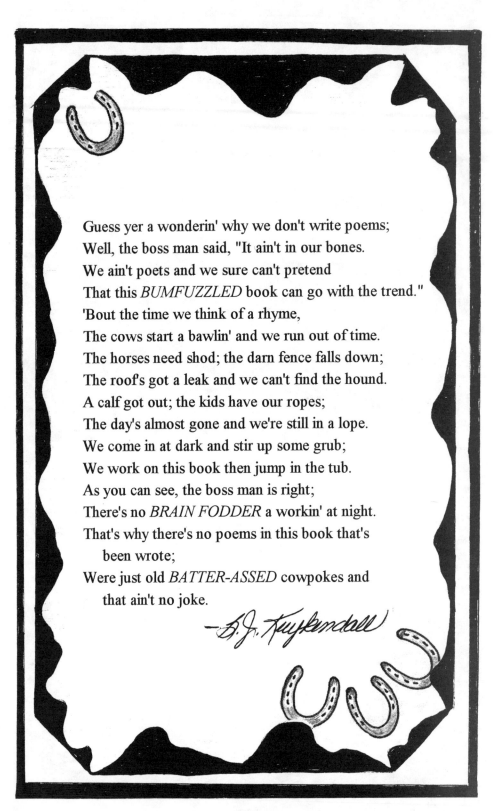

Guess yer a wonderin' why we don't write poems;

Well, the boss man said, "It ain't in our bones.

We ain't poets and we sure can't pretend

That this *BUMFUZZLED* book can go with the trend."

'Bout the time we think of a rhyme,

The cows start a bawlin' and we run out of time.

The horses need shod; the darn fence falls down;

The roof's got a leak and we can't find the hound.

A calf got out; the kids have our ropes;

The day's almost gone and we're still in a lope.

We come in at dark and stir up some grub;

We work on this book then jump in the tub.

As you can see, the boss man is right;

There's no *BRAIN FODDER* a workin' at night.

That's why there's no poems in this book that's
    been wrote;

Were just old *BATTER-ASSED* cowpokes and
    that ain't no joke.

—B.J. Kuykendall

Cheyenne Frontier
Days
1938

MISS HELEN MCCARTY

Miss Frontier welcomes You

to

CHEYENNE FRONTIER DAYS

OFFICIAL PROGRAM

1897 CHEYENNE FRONTIER DAYS 1938
"THE DADDY OF 'EM ALL"

EDWARD T. STOREY, Announcer

JOHN BELL, Arena Director

1938 FRONTIER DAYS COMMITTEE
R. J. HOFMANN, Chairman

JAMES A. STOREY, Treasurer
A. W. TROUT, Parade
MAJOR H. E. FULLER, Military

I. R. TOWNSEND, Indians
E. R. SAEGART, Tickets
R. D. HANESWORTH, Secretary

ARENA OFFICIALS
John Bell
Ed McCarty
Vern Elliott
Chas. W. Hirsig
Paul Hanson

TRACK OFFICIALS:
Wm. G. Haas
C. A. Black
Cal Holliday

OFFICIAL TIMERS:
Wm. F. DeVere
George Storey
T. Blake Kennedy
F. W. Fitch

CLERK OF COURSE:
Morton Nisbet

OFFICIAL STARTER:
Alfred J. Mooney

PROGRAM AND CONTESTANTS:
Dan E. Rees

ARENA JUDGES:
Carl Arnold
Donald Nesbit
Earl Thode

All Live Stock for this show furnished by McCarty and Elliott of Chugwater, Wyoming
Public Address System by Gordon G. Moss Radioservice, Greeley, Colorado

Second Day of Show, Wednesday, July 27, 1938

Event No. 1—GRAND OPENING ENTRY AND PARADE OF CONTESTANTS.

Event No. 2—CALF RIDING FOR BOYS UNDER 16 YEARS OF AGE.

Hugh Hamm
Jim Hamm
Ralph Morrell
Eugene Foy
Vern Chambers

Paul O'Brien
Russell Carney
Fred McKay
Robert Turk
Dick Reed

Harold Anderson
Fred Henry
Sterling Dunbar
Gene Sutherland
Norman Epler

Event No. 3—In Arena. INFANTRY DRILL by "E" Company, 20th United States Infantry of Fort F. E. Warren, Wyoming. Commanded by Capt. Paul R. Taylor. Lieut. T. R. Kimpton.

Event No. 4—Out of Chutes. BRAHMA STEER RIDING CONTEST. Purse $500.00 and all entrance fees. Entrance Fee $10.00. Purse will be split into two day moneys of 30 per cent each and divided 40, 30, 20 and 10 per cent. Final money or the remaining 40 per cent of the purse, divided 40, 30, 20 and 10 per cent.

No. 175—Herman Linder on No. 53
No. 197—George Mills on No. 128
No. 206—Carl Dossey on No. 41
No. 211—Slim Van Tassel on No. 40
No. 214—Deward Ryon on No. 32
No. 188—Smoky Snyder on No. 17

No. 205—Jimmie McGee on No. 89
No. 209—Carl Dykes on No. 12
No. 213—Bob Estes on No. 19
No. 219—Les McKenzie on No. 31
No. 220—Hughie Long on No. 7

Event No. 5—In Arena. ARTILLERY DRILL by "B" Battery, 76th United States Field Artillery, Fort F. E. Warren, Wyoming. Commanded by Capt. E. M. Taylor and Capt. Charles Wesner; 1st Lieut. W. J. Ledward and 1st Sergt. H. L. Cooper.

Event No. 6—Out of Chutes. BAREBACK RIDING CONTEST. Purse $400.00 and all entrance fees. Entrance fee $10.00. Purse will be split into two day moneys of 30 per cent each and divided 40, 30, 20 and 10 per cent. Final money or the remaining 40 per cent of the purse, divided 40, 30, 20 and 10 per cent. Winner of this event will receive a Stetson hat through Sol's Western Ranchman Outfitters.

No. 126—Paul Crain
No. 188—Smoky Snyder
No. 204—Rock Parker
No. 208—Urban Doan
No. 220—Hughie Long
No. 150—Jim Whiteman

No. 192—Fritz Becker
No. 205—Jimmie McGee
No. 212—Cecil Henley
No. 214—Duard Ryon
No. 214—Duard Ryon
No. 223—Johnny Hagen

No. 185—Eddie Teglund
No. 198—Hank Mills
No. 206—Carl Dossey
No. 213—Bob Estes
No. 216—George McIntosh

Event No. 7—On Track. WORLD'S CHAMPIONSHIP COWBOYS' RELAY RACE. One and one-half miles. Purse $1,125.00 and all entrance fees. Entrance fee $20.00. Total purse divided into five day moneys of 20 per cent of total; this day money to be divided 60, 25 and 15 per cent.

Rider and String
No. 36—Frankie Burns on Burns
No. 109—Floyd Murphy on Thorne & Murphy
No. 134—Cy Gray on Gray

Rider and String
No. 95—Jimmie Wallis on E. H. Kratzer
No. 131—Ernest Doty on Doty
No. 157—Hank Grimsly on Grimsly

127

Event No. 8—In Arena. WORLD'S CHAMPIONSHIP CALF ROPING CONTEST. Purse $1,000.00 and all entrance fees. Entrance fee $50.00. Purse will be split into two day moneys of 30 per cent each and divided 40, 30, 20 and 10 per cent. Final money or the remaining 40 per cent of the purse divided 40, 30, 20 and 10 per cent. Trophies: Winner to receive a silver mounted bridle through the Union Stock Yards Company of Omaha, Nebraska, and three cellophane wrapped Plymouth Yacht Lariat Ropes from the Plymouth Cordage Company of North Plymouth, Massachusetts. Second and third places also receive Plymouth Yacht Lariat Ropes.

No. 11—Andy Juarequi	No. 16—Maynard Gaylor	No. 28—E. Pardee
No. 30—King Merritt	No. 33—Morris Laycock	No. 42—Jess Goodspeed
No. 60—Buddy May	No. 65—Tom Rhodes	No. 83—Herb Meyers
No. 88—Amie Gamblin	No. 90—Clyde Burk	No. 93—Ted Powers
No. 102—Pat Lewis	No. 113—Zack Sellers	No. 123—Jake McClure
No. 174—Floyd Peters	No. 184—Richard Merchant	No. 187—Everett Bowman
No. 193—John Bowman	No. 194—Juan Salinas	No. 195—Toots Mansfield
No. 199—Asberry Schell	No. 200—Dick Robbins	No. 207—Carl Shepard
No. 24—Everett Shaw	No. 202—Allen Holder	

Event No. 9—In Arena. WAGON TRAIN HOLD UP. Reenactment of a typical experience of our Pioneer forefathers in 1870.

Event No. 10—On Track. INDIAN BUCK RACE by the Sioux Indians of Pine Ridge, South Dakota Reservation.

Hobert Blue Horse	Cecil Brave Eagle	Billy Red Cloud	Oliver Red Cloud

Event No. 11—On Track. COWBOYS' POTATO RACE. Purse, $50.00 daily.

Event No. 12—In Arena. AMATEUR BUCKING CONTEST. Open to amateurs only. Purse $500.00 and all entrance fees. Entrance fee $10.00. Purse will be split into two day moneys of 30 per cent each and divided 40, 30, 20 and 10 per cent. Final money or the remaining 40 per cent of the purse divided 40, 30, 20 and 10 per cent. Trophies: Winner of this event receives a saddle presented by the Colorado and Southern - Burlington Railroad, a silver belt buckle of the John B. Stetson Company, bridle with a hand made silver bit through the Plains Hotel, a Ray Bell Stetson hat through Max J. Meyer. Second place receives one pair Western Boots by Western Boot Company through Sol's Western Ranchman Outfitters.

No. 4—Clifford Wilcox on 53, Sally Gooden	No. 203—Jack Johnston on 47, Miss Wyoming
No. 46—Roy Cox on 60, Country Butter	No. 210—Earl Zammerman on 65, Black Cat
No. 54—Melvin Dikeman on No. 29, Galeton	No. 217—Homer Gillen on 57, Manitou
No. 74—Ross Meek on 68, Tip Toe	No. 221—Frank Chitwood on No. 36, Chihuahua
No. 75—Walter Fates on 51, Easy	Paint
No. 106—Geo. House on 40, Molly Malone	No. 222—Mel Weasa on 46, Norwegian
No. 190—James Like on 31, Sin Sin	

Event No. 13—On Track. WORLD'S CHAMPIONSHIP COWBOYS' TRICK AND FANCY ROPING. Purse $500.00. Divided $200.00, $150.00, $100.00 and $50.00.

No. 14—Paul St. Croy	No. 162—Texas Trenton
No. 179—Chet Howell	No. 180—Lewis Tindall

Event No. 14. In Arena. WORLD'S CHAMPIONSHIP STEER BULLDOGGING CONTEST. Purse $1,200.00 and all entrance fees. Entrance fee $25.00. Purse will be split into two day moneys of 30 per cent each and divided 40, 30, 20 and 10 per cent. Final money or the remaining 40 per cent of the purse divided 40, 30, 20 and 10 per cent. Trophies: Winner of this event will receive a Stetson hat, a pair of Boots and Lariat Rope through the Calvert Distilleries Corporation, Relay, Maryland.

No. 10—Homer Pettigrew	No. 201—Mike Fisher	No. 81—Tex Doyle
No. 127—Chick Martindale	No. 19—Milt Moe	No. 151—Hub Whiteman
No. 177—Howard McCrory	No. 143—Dick Anderton	No. 193—John Bowman
	No. 187—Everett Bowman	

Event No. 15—On Track. COWGIRLS' HALF-MILE COW PONY RACE. Purse $50.00 daily and all entrance fees. Entrance fee $10.00. Purse divided 50, 30 and 20 per cent.

No. 18—Gladys Pattinson	No. 99—Billie Nixon	No. 136—Mrs. G. H. Randal
No. 85—Jessie Triplett	No. 103—Gean Allen	No. 145—Reva Gray

Event No. 16—Out of Chutes. WORLD'S CHAMPIONSHIP COWBOYS' BUCK-ING CONTEST. Purse $1,400.00 and all entrance fees. Entrance fee $25.00. Purse will be split into two day moneys of 30 per cent each, divided 40, 30, 20 and 10 per cent. Final money or the remaining 40 per cent divided 40, 30, 20 and 10 per cent. Trophies: Winner of first place in this event to receive silver mounted saddle through the courtesy of the Union Pacific Railway Company.

No. 7—Nick Knight on 143, Mr. Pettibone	No. 173—Pete Grubb on 58, Whitcomb Hill
No. 8—Burrel Mulky on 109, Slingin Sam	No. 176—Bob Slappert on 67, Blue Bonnett
No. 25—Bob Askin on 44, Cottonwood	No. 212—Cecil Henley on 4, Dollar
No. 116—Rube Hubbell on 86, T. B. Hill	No. 218—Doff Aber on 164, Max Meyer
No. 148—Paul Carney on 59, V8	No. 223—Johnny Hagen on 133, Wings

Event No. 17—On Track. MEN'S HALF-MILE HORSE RACE. Purse $50.00 and all entrance fees. Entrance fee $10.00. Purse to be divided 50, 30 and 20 per cent.

No. 104—Dean Turpitt	No. 186—John Cheeney	No. 128—Andy Black
No. 134—Roscoe Flores	No. 110—Riley Hiser	No. 105—H. Vincent
No. 115—R. King	No. 159—Galen Lane	No. 141—B. Turpitt
	No. 135—Charlie Williams	

Event No. 18—In Arena. WORLD'S CHAMPIONSHIP STEER ROPING CON-TEST. Purse $1,400.00 and all entrance fees. Entrance fee $100.00. Purse to be split into two day moneys of 30 per cent each and divided 40, 30, 20 and 10 per cent. Final money or the remaining 40 per cent of the purse divided 40, 30, 20 and 10 per cent. Trophies: Winner of this event will receive a gold 21 jewel combination watch and timer through the Plymouth Cordage Company of North Plymouth, Massachusetts, and one flower stamped roping saddle through the courtesy of the Fred Mueller Saddle Company of Denver, Colorado. Second and third places will receive Plymouth Yacht Lariat Ropes through the Plymouth Cordage Company.

No. 13—Hugh Bennett	No. 202—Allen Holder	No. 17—Darvin Parks
No. 23—Walt Marcum	No. 15—John Rhodes	No. 48—Ace Soward
No. 50—Billy Wilkinson	No. 30—King Merritt	No. 63—Buck Sorrels
No. 64—Bud Parker	No. 58—Tom Taylor	No. 123—Jake McClure
No. 149—Eddie McCarty	No. 122—John McIntyre	No. 184—Richard Merchant
No. 187—Everett Bowman	No. 28—E. Pardee	No. 194—Juan Salinas
No. 195—Toots Mansfield	No. 193—John Bowman	No. 200—Dick Robbins
	No. 199—Asberry Schell	

Event No. 19—On Track. INDIAN SQUAW RACE. By Sioux Indians from the Pine Ridge Indian Reservation, Pine Ridge, South Dakota.

Nancy Lone Woman	Dorothy Cloud Shield	Susanna Red Cloud	Letha Charges in the Village

Event No. 20—On Track. WORLD'S CHAMPIONSHIP COWGIRLS' AND COWBOYS' TRICK AND FANCY RIDING CONTEST. Girls' purse $500.00, divided $200.00, $150.00, $100.00 and $50.00. Winner of this event will receive a saddle blanket from Rio Bamba, Equador, South America, through the Casserole Dining Room. Mens' purse $500.00, divided $200.00, $150.00, $100.00 and $50.00. Winner of this event to receive a silver belt buckle through the Frontier Hotel.

Girl Riders—
No. 47—Vivian White
No. 76—Claire Thompson
No. 182—Juanita Howell
No. 183—Velda Tindall

Men Riders—
No. 14—Paul St. Croy
No. 44—Earl Strauss
No. 79—Joe Cook
No. 2—Don Wilcox
No. 179—Chet Howell
No. 180—Lewis Tindall
No. 181—Paul Bond
No. 215—Ross Holt

Event No. 21—On Track. INDIAN WAR DANCE by Sioux Indians from the Pine Ridge Indian Reservation, Pine Ridge, South Dakota.

Event No. 22—On Track. WORLD'S CHAMPIONSHIP DENVER POST COWGIRLS' RELAY RACE. One and one-half miles. Purse $1,375.00 and all entrance fees. Entrance fee $20.00. Total purse divided into five day moneys of 20 per cent of the total, this day money to be divided 45, 25, 15, 10 and 5 per cent. Trophies: Denver Post Loving Cup and Elizabeth Arden trophy through A. E. Roedel, Druggist.

Rider and String—
No. 18—Gladys Pattinson on Roberts String
No. 96—Jean Allen on E. H. Kratzer String
No. 97—Della Shriver on C. Stier String
No. 114—Reva Gray on E. S. Cordell String

Rider and String—
No. 117—Jean Creed on Bristol & Deming String
No. 146—Fay Dennis on George Pringle String
No. 99—Billie Nixon on Burton String

Event No. 23.—On Track. WILD HORSE RACE. Day money $100.00, divided 50, 25, 15 and 10 per cent.

No. 2—Marvin Pennington	No. 38—Raymond Seeley	No. 53—Bill Wakefield
No. 56—John Cook	No. 61—Lloyd Clawson	No. 68—E. A. Mueller
No. 70—Jim Haback	No. 72—Clarence Anderson	No. 91—Bill Jones
No. 94—Ernie Sawyers	No. 120—Al Garrett	No. 132—Bud Vaughn
No. 144—Kid Fletcher	No. 158—Henry Thode	No. 161—E. D. Casteele

Contestants—1938 Frontier Day's Show

1. Edwin Hillman, Grover, Colo.
2. Marvin Pennington, Bushnell, Nebr.
3. Johnny Byrne, Cheyenne
4. Clifford Wilcox, Saratoga
5. Bob Norman, Saratoga
6. Joe Thompson, Coweta, Okla.
7. Nick Knight, Cody
8. Burel Mulkey, Salmon, Idaho
9. Frank Finley, Phoenix, Ariz.
10. Homer Pettigrey, Clovis, N. M.
11. Andy Jaurequi, Newhall Calif.
12. Lawrence Conley, Casa Grande, Ariz.
13. Hugh Bennett, Ft. Thomas, Ariz.
14. Paul St. Croy, Chandler, Ariz.
15. John Rhodes, Sombrero Butte, Ariz.
16. Maynard Gaylor, Casa Grande, Ariz.
17. Darvin Parks, Casa Grande, Ariz.
18. Gladys Pattenson, Hulett
19. Milt Moe, Comanche, Okla.
20. Holloway Grace, Palm Dale, Calif.
21. Bob Haverty, Eldorado, Kan.
22. Alfred Hayhurst, Coalgate, Okla.
23. Wolf Marcum, Ada, Okla.
24. Everett Shaw, Stonewall, Okla.
25. Bob Askin, Ismay, Mont.
26. Turk Greenough, Red Lodge, Mont.
27. Foreman Faulkner, Pawhuska, Okla.
28. E. Pardee, LaMarr, Colo.
29. Ike Rude, Mangum, Okla.
30. King Merritt, Federal
31. Whitey Christian, Cheyenne
32. Irby Mundy, Shamrock, Tex.
33. Maurice Leycock, Wheatland
34. Dale Kennedy, Denver, Colo.
35. Dick Truitt, Stonewall, Okla.
36. Frank Burns, Alamosa, Colo.
37. Art Casteel, Cheyenne
38. Raymond Seeley, Blythe, Calif.
39. Jack McWiggin, Williams, Ariz.
40. Glenn Soward, Buffalo, Okla.
41. Buck Goodspeed, Okemah, Okla.
42. Jess Goodspeed, Okemah, Okla.
43. Goldie Corbin, Ft. Worth, Tex.
44. Earl Strauss, Rockford, Ill.
45. Jimmie Hazen, Los Angeles, Calif.
46. Roy Cox, Reno, Nev.
47. Vivian White, Ringwood, Okla.
48. Ace Soward, Buffalo, Okla.
49. Johnnie Faris, Cheyenne
50. Billy Wilkinson, Cheyenne
51. Hugh Clingman, Prescott, Ariz.
52. G. W. Cox, Wagner, Ariz.
53. Bill Wakefield, Denver, Colo.
54. Melvin Dikeman, Hershey, Nebr.
55. Roy Chilcote, Cheyenne
56. John Cook, Cheyenne
57. Woodrow Chilcote, Cheyenne
58. Tom Taylor, Spafford, Tex.
59. Dee Burk, Comanche, Okla.
60. Buddy May, Nowata, Okla.
61. Lloyd Clawson, Cheyenne
62. Maurice Reilly, Maxwell, Nebr.
63. Buck Sorrells, Tucson, Ariz.
64. Bud Parker, Tucson, Ariz.
65. Tom Rhodes, Tucson, Ariz.
66. Vern Meeks, Big Piney
67. Melvin Pennington, Cheyenne
68. E. A. Mueller, Cheyenne
69. Earl Anderson, Divide
70. Jim Habeck, Cheyenne
71. Wallace Newton, Cheyenne
72. Clarence Anderson, Divide
73. Buck Standifer, Alton, Tex.
74. Ross Meeks, Big Piney
75. Walter Fates, Moran
76. Claire Thompson, Ft. Worth, Texas
77. Red Thompson, Comanche, Okla.
78. Joe Thompson, Comanche, Okla.
79. Joe Cook, Trinidad, Colo.
80. Stanley Furrow, Gill, Okla.
81. Tex Doyle, Pampa, Texas
82. Don Wilcox, Tulsa, Okla.
83. Herb Meyers, Okmulgee, Okla.
84. Jim Snively, Pawhuska, Okla.
85. Jessie Triplett, Greeley, Colo.
86. Francis Johnson, Divide
87. Roy Sewalt, Ft. Worth, Tex.
88. Amye Gamblin, Petrileo, Tex.
89. Jiggs Burk, Comanche, Okla.
90. Clyde Burk, Comanche, Okla.
91. Bill Jones, Federal
92. Harold Clawson, Cheyenne
93. Ted Powers, Osona, Texas
94. Ernie Sawyer, Cheyenne
95. Jimmie Wallis, Loveland, Colo.
96. Jean Allen, Larkspur, Colo.
97. Della Shriver, Riverside, Calif.
98. W. A. Philpot, Stapleton, Nebr.
99. Billie Nixon, Cheyenne
100. Roy Large, Ft. Washakie
101. Roy Lewis, House, N. M.
102. Pat Lewis, House, N. M.
103. Jean Allen, Larkspur, Colo.
104. Dean Turpitt, Crook, Colo.
105. H. Vincent, House, N. M.
106. Geo. House, Laramie
107. Jack Deming, Victor, Colo.
108. P. Domenquez, Montevista, Colo.
109. Floyd Murphy, Rye, Colo.
110. Riley Hiser, Steamboat Springs, Colo.
111. Tex Slocum, Denver, Colo.
112. Raymond Quigg, Del Rio, Texas
113. Jack Sellers, Del Rio, Texas
114. Reva Gray, Durango, Colo.
115. R. King, Tioga, Colo.
116. Rube Hubbell, Denver, Colo.
117. Gene Creed, Steamboat Springs, Colo.
118. Bob Crosby, Roswell, N. M.
119. Carl Arnold, Buckeye, Ariz.
120. Al Garrett, Alliance, Nebr.
121. Fred Lowry, Lenepah, Okla.
122. John McIntire, Lenepah, Okla.
123. Jake McClure, Lovington, N. M.
124. Cecil Owsley, Magdalena, N. M.
125. Bill Hortono, Buffalo, Wyo.
126. Paul Crain, Grover, Colo.
127. Chick Martindale, Oakley, Idaho
128. Andy Black, Oak Creek, Colo.
129. Black Blackborn, Cheyenne
130. Mrs. L. Hoskinson, Oak Creek, Colo.
131. Ernest Doty, Sargent, Nebr.
132. Bud Vaughn, Cheyenne
133. Charlie Bennett, Lusk
134. Cy Gray, Durango, Colo.
135. Chas. Williams, Wheatland
136. Mrs. G. J. Randall, Torrington, Wyo.
137. Roscoe Flores, Torrington
138. Jim Wilkinson, Meridan
139. Jim Laycock, Chugwater
140. D. Wallace, Oshkosh, Nebr.
141. B. Turpitte, Oshkosh, Nebr.
142. Walt Federer, Cheyenne
143. Dick Anderton, Ft. Worth, Texas
144. Kid Fletcher, Hugo, Colo.
145. Reva Grey, Oshkosh, Nebr.
146. Fay Dennis, Oshkosh, Nebr.
147. Fritz Truan, Long Beach, Calif.
148. Paul Carney, Galeton, Colo.
149. Ed McCarty, Chugwater
150. Jim Whitemore, Clarksville, Texas
151. Hub Whiteman, Clarksville, Texas
152. Cliff Helm, Dallas, Texas
153. Harold Piper, Jelm, Wyo.
154. Jeff Lass, Glenrock, Wyo.
155. Ward Watkins, Thatcher, Colo.
156. Geo. Patterson, Silver City, N. M.
157. Hank Grimsley, Swink, Colo.
158. Henry Thode, Black Diamond, Alberta, Canada
159. Gaylen Lane, Johnson, Kan.
160. J. R. Chilcote, Laramie
161. Ed Casteele, Cheyenne
162. Texas Trenton, Washington, D. C.
163. Bill Cox, Belle Fourche, S. D.
164. Pete Sorenson, Nisland, S. D.
165. Tommy Williams, Silver City, N. M.
166. John Jordan, Florence, Ariz.
167. Pete Palmer, Cheyenne
168. Ralph Lanning, Cheyenne
169. Rusty McGinty, Plains, Tex.
170. Tom Hogan, Tulsa, Okla.
171. Eddie Curtis, ElReno, Okla.
172. Vick Schwartz, Wichita Falls, Tex.
173. Pete Grubb, Salmon, Idaho
174. Floyd Peters, Browning, Mont.
175. Herman Linder, Cardston, Alberta, Canada
176. Dick Slappert, Miles City, Mont.
177. Howard McCrorey, Deadwood, S. D.
178. Billy Kingham, Cheyenne
179. Chet Howell, Lysite, Wyo.
180. Louis Tindall, Ft. Worth, Texas
181. Paul Bond
182. Juanita Howell
183. Velda Tindall, Ft. Worth, Texas
184. Richard Merchant, Tucson, Ariz.
185. Eddie Teglund, Cody
186. John Cjeeney, Greeley, Colo.
187. Everett Bowman, Hillside, Ariz.
188. Smoky Snyder, Buena Park, Calif.
189. V. Wallis, Johnson, Kan.
190. James Like, Kim, Colo.
191. S. I. Fernandez, Monte Vista, Colo.
192. Fritz Becker, Alamosa, Colo.
193. John Bowman, Oakdale, Calif.
194. Juan Salinas, Encimal, Tex.
195. Toots Mansfield, Bandera, Tex.
196. Frankie Allen, Larkspur, Colo.
197. George Mills, Montrose, Colo.
198. Hank Mills, Montrose, Colo.
199. Asberry Schell, Tempe, Ariz.
200. Rick Robbins, Tempe, Ariz.
201. Mike Fisher, Dunning, Neb.
202. Allen Holder, Sheffield, Tex.
203. Jack Johnston, Grand Island, Neb.
204. Rock Parker, Waco, Tex.
205. Jimmie McGee, Phoenix, Ariz.
206. Cary Dossey, Phoenix, Ariz.
207. Carl Sheffield, Payson, Ariz.
208. Urban Doan, Alberta, Canada
209. Carl Dykes, Ft. Worth, Tex.
210. Earl Zammerman, Split Rock
211. Slim Van Tassel, Lusk
212. Cecil Henley, Hayward, Calif.
213. Bob Estes, Baird, Tex.
214. Duward Ryon, Duncan, Okla.
215. Ross Holt, Evanston, Wyo.
216. George McIntosh, Calgary, Canada
217. Meyer Sillen, St. Louis, Mo.
219. Les McKenzie, Douglas, Wyo.
220. Hughie Long, Cresson, Tex.
221. Frank Chitwood, Billings, Mont.
222. Mel Weasa, Wolf Point, Mont.
223. Johnny Hagen, Wolf Point, Mont.

130

CTA

COWBOYS WOULDN'T HATE
MATHMATICS SO BAD IF IT WASN'T
FER ALL THE DANG NUMBERS....

YA CAN'T GET TO GOIN' 'TILL YA STICK YER NECK OUT

This caption was the philosophy of the rodeo cowboys when they first organized. It has been said that another reason they adopted the symbol of the turtle, was that they intended to move slow and sure in the initial stages of their new movement, and once they "took hold", they would be hell to knock loose.

The official emblem of the Cowboys Turtle Association, organized in 1936. The Turtle Button, that was issued to CTA members, became a very sentimental item to those who wore it. They usually displayed it either on their hat or belt. The story has been told that Fritz Truan, a champion saddle bronc rider of the 1930's, lost his Turtle Button on the battle field during World War II. Upon discovering the loss while in the safety of shell fire, he immediately risked his life; crawled back on the battle field and retrieved his treasured badge.

For the Boston Show, we the undersigned demand that the Purses
be doubled and the Entrance Fees added in each and every event.
Any Contestant failing to sign this Petition will **not** be permitted
to contest, by order of the undersigned.

[handwritten signatures of rodeo cowboys]

FROM A LITTLE ACORN THE OAK TREE GREW

This is the first official document of organization of professional rodeo cowboys. It came about because Col. W.T. Johnson, one of the noted producers of some of the bigger rodeos, had the cowboys competing for "Peanuts."

The cowboys had tried to negotiate with the Colonel for larger purses to no avail. Therefore, they organized by signing this agreement at the Boston Garden in October, 1936. They proclaimed that at least their entrance fees would be added to the purses or they would strike.

The Colonel's reponse was, "strike and be damned." That they did.... the signers of this, their new constitution, walked out into the middle of Boston Garden and sat down. The manager of the Garden then told the Colonel to "get right" and put on a show or the promised monies for the rodeo would be forfeited. The Colonel wilted, settled with the cowboys, and the show went on.

This was the stepping stone for orderly negotiations between the Colonel and the cowboys for what amount of monies they would work for at all rodeos in the future. The cowboys formed the Cowboy Turtle Association, adopting the name and the symbol of the turtle as their trade mark. The turtle was chosen because they felt they had been so slow in getting around to having a voice in rodeo affairs.

The "Turtles" went on to become a successful force in the future development of professional rodeo. They remained effective under this title until the name was changed in 1945 to the Rodeo Cowboys Association. The name of the organization was changed again in 1974 to the Professional Rodeo Cowboys Association, and has operated under that title ever since.

THEY GOT THE TURTLES GOIN'

Hugh Bennett and Everett Bowman in 1937 at Madison
Square Garden Rodeo in New York City, N.Y.

IF YA REACH HARD ENOUGH FOR YOUR DREAMS... IT CAN HAPPEN

Lois and Everett Bowman with Josie and Hugh Bennett

Hugh Bennett of Falcon, Colorado and Everett Bowman of Hillside, Arizona, brothers-in-law, were the big cogs that got the Cowboy's Turtle Association in gear in 1936.

Everett as president and Hugh as secretary-treasurer, along with their sister wives, Lois and Josie, were the ones who made it tick. The men signed the cowboys up and kicked 'em straight, (sometimes literally!) The sisters kept the books and the money in the back seat of their car and did the office work.

When the organization ultimately evolved into the Professional Rodeo Cowboys Association in 1944, these four makers of history retired from administrative duties.

COWBOY TURTLES ASSOCIATION BANQUET

COWBOY TURTLES ASSOCIATION BANQUET,
Hotel Texas, Fort Worth, March, 7, 1940

A COWBOY'S CHEWIN' APPARATUS PLAIN
WON'T WORK WITH HIS HAT ON IN A
PUBLIC RESTAURANT

Hotel Texas, Fort Worth, March 7, 1940

The Turtles moved "slow and sure"
and they "took hold."

THE QUALITY OF A PERSON'S LIFE IS IN DIRECT PROPORTION TO THEIR COMMITMENT TO EXCEL

FANNYE LOVELADY
Rodeo
Lady of the Year
1985

Fannye Lovelady of Dewey, Arizona, has certainly been one of a kind!

Fannye was raised in the cattle business in Texas, and came to Arizona at an early age. Married to Shorty Lovelady, they participated in pro rodeo in the days of the Cowboys Turtle Association and the early days of the Professional Rodeo Cowboys Association. From 1940 to 1944, she served as the only paid secretary that the Turtles ever had.

Now in her eighties, she remains very enthusiastic about rodeo, devoting endless time to all inquiries of those interested in the sport. A true historian of rodeo, she was an invaluable source in the accumulation of much of the CTA data in this book.

She has recently been awarded a Gold Card from the Professional Rodeo Cowboys Hall of Fame in Colorado Springs, Colorado. She is honored in the National Cowboy Hall of Fame in Oklahoma City, Oklahoma, where, also in 1985, she was awarded the Gold Medallion pictured here, as "Rodeo Lady of the Year".

I will forever be in debt to Fannye for supplying a copy of the CTA rule book, and other pro rodeo data.

"Thanks a million, Fannye... You're a Doll."

Author's note: While *Bumfuzzled* was in press, we learned of Fannye's passing on August 21, 1995. The rodeo world lost an irreplaceable friend and loyal supporter. We will never forget her.

THE
COWBOYS'
Turtle
ASSOCIATION

ARTICLES OF

ASSOCIATION

BY-LAWS AND RULES

1944

EVERETT BOWMAN .... President
Rt. 1, Box 451A, Tempe, Arizona

TOOTS MANSFIELD .... Vice-President
Box 546, Big Springs, Texas

FANNYE LOVELADY .... Secy.-Treasurer
733 West McDowell Rd., Phoenix, Arizona

DIRECTORS

LOUIS BROOKS .... Saddle Bronc Riding
Sweetwater, Texas

CLYDE BURK .... Calf Roping
Comanche, Oklahoma

EDDIE CURTIS .... Steer Wrestling
El Reno, Oklahoma

DICK GRIFFITH .... Contact Performers
Scottsdale, Arizona

KING MERRITT .... Steer Roping-Team Tying
Federal, Wyoming

GEORGE MILLS .... Bareback Riding
Montrose, Colorado

SMOKY SNYDER .... Bull Riding
Corona, California

SPOKESMEN

JERRY AMBLER, St. Helens, Oregon
STUB BARTLEMAY, White Salmon, Wash.
JOE BASSETT, Payson, Arizona
LEONARD BLOCK, Livermore, California
W. W. BOMAR, Clovis, New Mexico
PAUL CARNEY, Kirkland, Arizona
TOM COLEMAN, Walsenburg, Colorado
JACKIE COOPER, Newhall, California
CECIL CORNISH, Waukomis, Oklahoma
VERN GOODRICH, Newhall, California
J. K. HARRIS, Longview, Texas
CLYDE HERBERT, Beaumont, Texas
D. HINTON, Molalla, Washington
SHIRLEY HUSSEY, Moses Lake, Wash.
JAMES KINNEY, Marathon, Texas
ROY LEWIS, House, New Mexico
EMMETT LYNCH, Walla Walla, Wash.
VIC MONTGOMERY, Ozona, Texas
SHORTY McCROREY, Waverley, New York
FOX O'CALLAHAN, Newhall, California
JAUN SALINAS, Encinal, Texas
PAUL SCOTT, Pocatello, Idaho
GLEN SHAW, Eascalon, California
CHARLIE SMITH, Rifle, Colorado
JOHN TUBBS, Spokane, Washington
FRANK VAN METER, Weiser, Idaho
ORAL SUMALT, Wolf Creek, Montana

ADVISORY COMMITTEE
Francis J. Riley, Ethel M. Hopkins,
Jack Kriendler

143

ARTICLES OF ASSOCIATION

The undersigned hereby certify that:

FIRST:

The name of this Association is and shall be,

THE COWBOYS' TURTLE ASSOCIATION.

SECOND:

The Cowboys' Turtle Association (hereinafter sometimes referred to as the CTA) has been formed for the following purposes:

1. To organize the professional rodeo contestants of the U. S. A. for their mutual protection and benefit.
2. To raise the standards of cowboy contests, so they rank among the foremost American sports.
3. To co-operate, insofar as possible, with the management of all rodeos at which the members contest.
4. To protect members against unfairness on the part of any rodeo management.
5. To bring about honest advertising by the rodeo associations, so that the public may rely upon the truth of advertised events in which it is claimed that members of the CTA will participate.
6. To work for the betterment of conditions and of the rules governing rodeo events in which the members of the CTA take part.
7. To establish a central place for registration for the convenience of members.
8. To publish information concerning the dates of rodeos, the names of contestants, the prize money, and other particulars in which members are interested.
9. To create a fund to be used in case of death for the benefit of members who have completed their payments to the CTA.

MEMBERSHIP

THIRD:

Members shall be such professional rodeo participants as are provided in the bylaws.

MEETINGS

FOURTH:

1. A General Meeting shall be held one in each calendar year in Cheyenne, Wyo., to nominate three contestants from each of the 7 events specified in the by-laws to be voted upon by ballot for election to the Board of Directors.
2. Three candidates from each of the 7 events may be nominated at other meetings of the members, held at such places as may be designated by the Board, as provided in the by-laws.
3. An Annual Meeting of the members of the CTA shall be held once in each calendar year at New York city for the announcement of the election of directors and the transaction of business. The Board of Directors shall make a full report of their activities during the preceding fiscal year, and recommend such measures for the future as they may think advisable; and the new board shall also report their election of officers.
4. A quorum at a general meeting shall be twenty-five members, and at an annual meeting shall be fifty.

FIFTH:

The President may call a meeting of the Board of Directors at any time, provided each members is given advance notice of the meeting.

SIXTH:

Any three directors may also call a meeting, giving similar notice

SEVENTH:

If the by-laws or rules are to be amended, a minimum of two days' notice must be given, stating the purpose of the meeting.

EIGHTH:

Members shall present their cards of membership upon ending a CTA meeting upon request of a director or spokesman.

BOARD OF DIRECTORS

NINTH:

1. The Board of Directors shall consist of eight members—the President ex-officio and seven members, one to represent each of seven events.
2. The Board of Directors may appoint Spokesmen in different territories to aid the CTA in negotiations when the directors are not present. In case there is only the spokesman present he is to take the matter in question up with all of the boys present.
3. Both directors and spokesmen shall aid the Treasurer in the collection of dues and fines owed by the contestants where unable to send to main office.

TENTH:

At all meetings of the Board, four directors shall constitute a quorum.

144

ELEVENTH:

The legislative or rule-making power of the CTA shall be held by the Board of Directors. It shall have general supervision over the business and affairs of the Association; with the power to make, adopt, alter or amend the by-laws as hereinafter specified. It may make all rules which is considers necessary to carry out the purposes of this organization, and any contracts incidental thereto.

OFFICERS

TWELFTH:
1. The officers of the CTA shall be as follows:
   President, Vice-President, Secretary and Treasurer
   They shall be elected by the Board of Directors at the time of the annual meeting to serve for the period of one year or until their successors are elected.
2. The **President** shall preside at all meetings of the CTA and of the Board of Directors. He shall enforce all rules and regulations of the CTA and perform such other duties as shall be assigned to him by the Board of Directors.
3. In the absence or disability of the President, the **Vice-President** shall perform his duties.
4. The **Secretary** shall keep the minutes and other official reports of the CTA. He shall conduct its official correspondence and shall keep all records, books, documents and papers relating to the CTA at such place as shall be designated by the Board of Directors.
5. The **Treasurer** shall keep account of all money received by him and shall deposit it in the name of the CTA in such depository as shall be designated by the Board of Directors. He shall not pay out or disburse any of the money of the CTA except by check, which must be signed by the President, or in case of his death, disability or absence, by the Vice-President, and countersigned by the Secretary of the CTA. At each annual meeting of the members he shall make a statement of the current financial condition of the CTA and a detailed report of its condition for the preceding fiscal year. The Treasurer shall be bonded.
6. The **President** shall be a member of the Board of Directors ex-officio but any of the above mentioned officers, other than the President, may also be elected members of the Board, and shall serve as Representatives of their events as well.
7. All officers and directors shall serve without salary or other compensation, except Secretary-Treasurer.
8. Officers, directors and spokesmen may be removed at any time with or without (legal) cause by a majority vote of the Board of Directors.
9. Resignations of officers, directors and spokesmen must be presented to the Board of Directors and be accepted by a majority vote of those present and voting before they become final.
10. The Board of Directors may fill any vacancy among the officers, directors or spokesmen by vote of the majority of those present and voting at any meeting. Such election to be for the unexpired term.
11. Any locality can petition for a spokesman if local conditions demand such action. In such a case the spokesman petitioned for must be passed on by the Board of Directors.

AMENDMENTS

THIRTEENTH:
The Articles of Association may be amended at any time at any annual or general meeting of the members of the CTA by the vote of a majority of the members present, provided there is a quorum.

BY-LAWS
NOMINATION AND ELECTIONS TO THE BOARD OF DIRECTORS

1. Three candidates shall be nominated at the general meeting in Cheyenne (Wyo.) or, an additional three, at the discretion of the Board of Directors, may be nominated at general meetings held at such places as may be designated by the Board. The three candidates from each event receiving the most votes shall be nominated for office.
3. The names of the candidates nominated at this meeting shall be published in the September issue of Hoofs and Horns magazine edited by Ma Hopkins of Tucson, Arizona, which is the official CTA publication. They shall be voted upon at the annual meeting held in New York City.

145

4. Each CTA member in good standing shall be entitled to cast one vote for a director chosen from the event or events in which he contests. The candidates receiving the highest number of votes shall constitute of the Board of Directors for the ensuing year.

5. Members, who cannot be present at the meeting in New York, shall mail their votes before October first to the Secretary. These ballots shall be counted and the results announced at the annual meeting.

6. Each member shall write his full name and address on his ballot; other wise it will not be accepted or counted.

MEMBERSHIP AND DUES

1. Membership in the CTA is confined to professional rodeo contestants and rodeo contract performers. This is to include cowgirl bronc riders, trick riders, trick ropers, clowns, announcers, and other contract performers that are considered a pertinent part of the rodeo.
   a. All above mentioned contract performers must be members of the CTA, and cannot work any show where CTA members are barred.
   b. Contract performers may be fined or suspended or both, at the discretion of the Board of Directors.
   c. Contract performers, however, may not accept contracts after the CTA serves notice that is members will be withdrawn from a given rodeo.

2. Eligibility for membership in the CTA shall be left to the discretion of the directors, officers or spokesmen of said organization.
   a. Members of the CTA will refuse to contest at any rodeo with cowboys who, having qualified as professionals, have not joined the CTA.
   b. And director or spokesman or officers shall have authority to inform rodeo managements as to which contestants have qualified as professionals but have not yet joined the CTA.
   c. If the rodeo management permits such a contestant to enter, the CTA reserves the right to withdraw its members from competition.

3. Annual dues of membership are hereby fixed at ten dollars a year.

4. Annual dues shall be payable before entering the first rodeo of the season at which a member contests.

5. Any members who does not pay his dues by March 15th of each year whether he has contested or not is automatically suspended. To be reinstated, said member must have the approval of the Board of Directors.

6. Any member of the CTA who has not paid his dues for 1941, or any year previous to that, will be dropped from the list of CTA members and will not be permitted to contest at any rodeo. To be reinstated such a member must pay all back dues in full, plus 10 dollars for each year in which said dues have not been paid.

7. Dues for cowgirl bronc riders who do nothing but ride broncs are five dollars per year.

8. Should any member of the CTA be taken into the Armed Forces soon after paying their dues shall have their dues refunded upon written request to the CTA office. CTA members in service shall be issued membership cards good for the duration without pay.

9. Only members in good standing shall vote in the affairs of the CTA. No member who is in default as to payments for dues or fines, and no member who is at the time suspended, will be permitted to vote.

10. The CTA, through its Board of Directors, shall adopt a card certifying the contestant's or contract performer's membership in the Association.

11. Election to honorary membership in the CTA shall be subject to the approval of a member of the Board of Directors, a Spokesman, or officers. Honorary members shall be given cards and insignia which differ from those of regular members. Annual dues for honorary members are hereby fixed at five dollars. Honorary members are not eligible to vote.

12. An Advisory Committee may be appointed by the majority of the Board of Directors to serve the CTA in an advisory capacity for the period of one year, or until they are succeeded. Members of the Advisory Committee are not eligible to vote.

13. By-laws and rules may be amended by a majority vote of the Board of Directors.

RULES

1. **No CTA member shall contest at any amateur rodeo.**

2. Rodeo stock contracts cannot furnish stock to both professional and amateur shows. If a stock contractor furnishes stock to an amateur show, they must stay amateur.

3. Stock Contractors are requested to make sure all prize lists have been approved by the CTA before signing a contract to furnish stock for a show.

4. No CTA member shall be allowed to contest at any rodeo unless the entry fees for each event are added to the guaranteed prize money of each event.
   a. No rodeo shall be responsible for returning a contestant's entry fees if he has contested in an event even once during the show. But if he is entered in other events in which he is unable to contest, the entry fees for those events must be returned.

5. No CTA member shall be allowed to contest at any rodeo unless competition is open to all members of the CTA in good standing.
   a. Therefore, no CTA member shall contest at any rodeo which places penalties or handicaps upon CTA members.
   b. No CTA member shall contest at any amateur rodeo or state championships or in special, closed, or amateur events. However, a rodeo having special events for local talent, shall not be classified as an amateur rodeo by virtue of that fact alone.
   c. If a rodeo has a special day for amateur contests, no CTA member shall be permitted to contest.

6. If more than two events are held a show will not be considered a jack pot, and to qualify as a jack pot contest must be OK'd by CTA.

7. Open rodeo contests must be CTA and members cannot participate in contract or closed shows.

8. If an Amateur event is held in a professional show a like event must be held for the professionals.

9. No CTA member shall be allowed to ride for mount money unless a contest in the event is included in said rodeo's program.

   a. However, if five or less contestants are entered in an event, CTA members may ride, rope or wrestle for mount money.

10. No CTA member shall be allowed to contest at any rodeo unless the judges are experienced men, shall have been passed upon by the three riding representatives of the CTA, and are satisfactory to a majority of the Board of Directors of the CTA.

11. If a rodeo hires its judges in advance, the names of the judges chosen must be submitted to the CTA for approval before they are printed on said rodeo's prize list.
    a. If a rodeo prints the names of judges on its prize list without having submitted them to the CTA for approval, the CTA reserves the right to withdraw its members from contesting under said judges.
    b. If a rodeo does not hire its judges in advance the rodeo committee may select competent men who shall be passed upon by the CTA members entered at said rodeo.
    c. Timers and flagmen must be men of experience. If the CTA does not consider the men chosen by a given rodeo to have adequate experience, they will expect co-operation from the management in replacing the unsatisfactory timers or flagmen.
    d. The decisions of the judges, flagmen and timers who have been passed upon by the CTA shall be final, and no protest by the contestants will be permitted.

12. The CTA agrees to adopt the RAA rules for rodeo contests and will insist that rodeo managements adhere to them.

13. Any member of the CTA who does not observe the above rules is liable to a fine, suspension, or both.

14. The CTA reserves the right to withdraw their members from competition in any rodeo which does not conform to the above rules or which refuses to co-operate with the Turtle Association in the arbitration of difficulties.

PENALTIES FOR INFRACTION OF RULES

1. **Any member of the CTA who contests, performs or works at a rodeo which as been boycotted by the CTA is liable to a fine, suspension, or both.**

2. Any CTA member guilty of misconduct will be notified to appear before the Board of Directors for a meeting and if proven guilty of misconduct will be suspended—or fined—or both.
   a. If the Board sees fit, it may advance payment for outstanding bills incurred by members during a given rodeo.
   b. Members shall not be reinstated unless the CTA is repaid.
3. Any member who wishes to resign from the CTA must do so in writing. A member who withdraws in good faith shall be reinstated without fine or penalty, provided he has not contested, worked or performed at any rodeo during the time in which his resignation took effect.
   a. In case a member has contested, worked or performed at a rodeo during the period of his resignation and wishes to be reinstated, he shall be fined, suspended or both, according to the discretion of the Board of Directors before he shall be reinstated.
4. Any member who falsely represents himself as qualified to speak for the CTA shall be fined, suspended or both to the limit of the power of the Board of Directors.
   a. **The President, the representatives (Directors) or the spokesmen are the only members of the organization who have authority to make decisions for the CTA.**
   b. Certain members will carry letters from the Board of Directors authorizing them to collect dues, take in new members and collect bad bills.
5. Any member of the CTA who has a grievance against the organization shall present same to the representative of his event or to a spokesman. Any member who wilfully causes trouble inside or outside the ranks of the CTA shall be liable to a fine, suspension, or both.
6. Any member of the CTA who denies his membership and removes his CTA button on entering a rodeo, shall be fined to the fullest extent within the power of the Board of Directors.
7. Any member who makes himself liable to a fine must pay the same or post a bond of fifty dollars ($50.00) with the Secretary of the CTA until he has had a hearing before the Board of Directors.
8. If the Board of Directors finds him guilty, by the majority vote of all the Directors, he may be fined from $25.00 to $500.00 at their discretion, or suspended, or both.
9. Any member of the CTA who has been fined and fails to pay one-quarter of his winnings at the time the prize money is won until the fine is paid, is liable to be expelled from the CTA and shall forfeit any part or portion of the fine he has already paid.
   a. Any contract performer who has been fined and fails to pay one-quarter of each contract at the time said contact is paid, until the fine is paid in full, is liable to be expelled from the CTA and shall forfeit any part or portion of the fine he has already paid.
10. It is understood that no officer, director, member, or employee of the CTA, shall be liable individually or other wise for any breach of the above rules, or for any understanding or agreement between the CTA and RAA or with any other rodeo association.
11. If the Rodeo Management furnishes feed for contestants' horses the CTA urges each member to ride in Grand Entries and Parades, and will sanction the fines placed by management for non-cooperation.

POLICY

It is the policy of the CTA that each member present at a given rodeo shall attend all general meetings of the CTA.

The CTA reserves the right to withdraw its members from competition if the prize money is too unequally divided.

If a rodeo management wishes absolute guarantee that members of the CTA will participate at a given rodeo after their arrival at said rodeo, they must submit their prize list for approval not later than thirty days prior to show dates to the main office of the Cowboys' Turtle Association, Phoenix, Arizona.

The CTA shall be responsible for seeing that all approved prize lists shall be signed by at least three directors (representatives) and the President or four Directors.

EVERETT BOWMAN
President

148

MEMBERS OF THE CTA

Number	Name	Number	Name
1388	Acay, Delmar	H308	Bell, John H.
1631	Adair, Pud	452	Bender, Bennie
342	Adams, Dale	8	Bennett, Hugh
1206	Adams, Pete	338	Beren, John
146	Ahern, Buck	499	Berry, Padgett
309	Akers, Ves	207	Betts, Glenn M.
1871	Allen, Del	1682	Billingsley, Red
367	Allen, Frankie	440	Bland, R. L., Jr.
578	Allen, Hoss	94	Blasingame, Jack
2018	Allen, Jean	1680	Blessing, Wag
245	Allen, Red	1610	Block, Leonard
1850	Almond, John	112	Bode, Andrew
496	Alrich, H.A.	1620	Boen, Ken
1445	Alrich, Hank	63	Boen, Mrs. Ken
1142	Alsbough, Walt	1772	Bomar, W. W.
471	Altamarino, Tony	395	Bond, Paul
227	Alvord, Fred	101	Booth, Clinton
286	Ambler, Jerry	1028	Booth, Homer R.
170	Anderson, Dick	797	Border, Alex
2008	Anderson, Dick	766	Boss, Ray
379	Armstrong, Ted	273	Bowen, Glenn W.
70	Arnold, Carl	551	Bowman, Ed
891	Arrants, Gener	15	Bowman, Everett
432	Autry, Frank	10	Bowman, John
1940	Axton, Bob	76	Bowyer, Chester
1601	Bacon, Grant	403	Boyd, Tom
1691	Bacon, John	1453	Brady, Buff, Jr.
1405	Badsky, Fred	312	Brady, Pat
1787	Bailey, Herb	1348	Branch, Riley
404	Baker, J. Howard	485	Bride, Tom
24	Baker, Paddy	375	Brister, Jim
372	Ballard, Smokey	583	Broderick, John
1944	Barens, Roy	850	Brodnax, Chas.
1566	Barmby, Bob	975	Brooks, Louis
789	Barnett, Ernie	178	Brown, Basil
141	Barrett, Fred	187	Brown, Howard
89	Barlemay, Stub	958	Brown, Jerry
564	Bassett, Joe	332	Brown, Pat
2022	Baughman, Wart	276	Brown, W.H. 'Tex'
540	Becker, Fritz	325	Browne, Robert
287	Bedford, Cecil	177	Brunton, Carol
273	Belden, Herb	388	Buetler, Lynn

515	Buffington, Ernest	200	Colborn, Rose Mary
1111	Bugg,Johnnie	1156	Collier, Ralph
743	Burk, Jiggs	521	Collins, Earvin
144	Burke, Clyde	510	Connell, Junio
1821	Burleson, W. E.	609	Cook, Bud
1882	Burns, Bobbie	48	Cooper, Jackie
1667	Burrough, George	837	Cornish, Cecil
1049	Burrows, Bob	374	Cotrell, Lyle
498	Butts, Buster	44	Cox, Breezy
1209	Byers, Chester	696	Cox, Frank
2004	Cabral, Louis	167	Cripe, A. J.
1629	Cahoe, Tommy	72	Cropper, Melvin
191	Caldwell, Eddie	185	Crobsy, Bob
386	Campbell, Arlo	212	Curry, Roland
308	Campbell, A.J. (Jack)	122	Curtis, Andy
1729	Capps, Kenneth	132	Curtis, Eddie
331	Carey, Lawrence	119	Dahl, Herb
21	Carney, Paul	324	Dahlberg, Shorty
315	Carson, Ken	302	Daniels, Larry
373	Castanon, Frank	433	Daniels, Robert F.
253	Casteel, Art	1374	Darnell, Fred
1684	Castro, Vern	253	Davis, Harold
396	Cavanaugh, Tommy	1716	Davis, Merle
1556	Cavender, Eugene	1980	Deakins, Ab.
360	Chaffie, Jim	483	Dee, Clarence
1894	Chapman, John	168	Del R, M. W.
461	Charles, Artie	1155	Demaree, George
790	Chesson, Bo	556	Dikeman, Melvin
1119	Chitwood, Frank	1710	Dillon, Mutt
2016	Christensen, Bobie	1226	Dixon, Eddie
1880	Christensen, Henry	174	Dixon, Homer
934	Christian, Lefty	1346	Dossey, Bernice
456	Clayton, Tommy	204	Dossey, Carl
202	Clemans, W. J.	1204	Doucet, Poley
258	Cline, Doc	828	Dowelll, Buck
255	Cline, George	1218	Dreyer, Polly
1131	Cline, John	241	Drowne, Skip
1989	Cline, Lawrence	1736	Duarte, Ed
430	Cline, Leck	1276	Dugger, Bufard
74	Clingman, Hugh	1048	Dunbar, Marvin
223	Coats, Bobby	1734	Durfee, Tex
252	Coelho, Al (Louis)	949	Dyer, Jack
571	Coker, Joe	104	Echols, Buck
1582	Colborn, Everett	1833	Edmonson, Lince

152	Edwards, Joe	487	Gerig, John
1568	Edwards, Sonny	54	Getzwiller, Marion
1938	Ellingwalt, P. W.	192	Gill, Emmett
1997	Elliot, Cliff	156	Glade, Pete
1956	Elliott, Verne	1966	Glatfelder, Gene
1597	Emerson, Tex	1430	Glenn, Dick
481	Enders, Bob	1772	Glenn, Lester
1035	Enos, Manuel	2017	Golia, Philip
1865	Espy, Jim	1537	Goodrich, Myrtle
362	Estes, Bob	1538	Goodrich, Vern
1828	Evans, Bert	263	Goodspeed, Buck
219	Evans, Floyd James	645	Gould, Pauul
215	Facciola, Don B.	13	Grace, Halloway
415	Falk, Dr. Lane	90	Graham, J. A.
813	Fancher, Sam	123	Graham, Kenneth
1847	Farnsworth, Dick	1236	Gray, Juanita
314	Farr, Carl	1237	Gray, Weaver
316	Farr, Hugh	1141	Green, Carlos
470	Farris, Zeano	1539	Green, Ray
1223	Favors, Jack	668	Greenough, Alice
543	Fernandez, Fele	669	Greenough, Margie
903	Fernandez, Ike	23	Greenough, Turk
414	Fidler, C. Lyall	289	Greenwood, Ross
476	Finley, Evelyn	3	Griffith, Dick
836	Finley, Larry	454	Gruwell, Gus
1798	Fischer, Charles H.	1830	Guidotti, Raymond Lloyd
1735	Flagg, Slim	65	Gunter, Kenneth
172	Flesher, Herbert	624	Guymon, Sandy
459	Fletcher, Claude	1937	Hale, Earl
557	Flowers, Hubert	1572	Hale, Mel
945	Flowers, Marshall	434	Hall, Clark
1763	Folsom, Barney	377	Hancock, Bill
480	Fomville, Paul	1744	Hannen, Chick
1774	Fort, Troy	1960	Hansen, Curt
1527	Fox, Dewey	1081	Hansen, Kenneth
1541	Frazier, Larry	1867	Hansen, Merrill
444	Freeman, E. J.	1954	Harper, Bert A.
1252	Fulkerson, Jasbo	1208	Harris, J. K.
173	Galbraith, Joe	246	Hart, Harry
229	Gale, Floyd	226	Hastings, Mike
350	Gamlin, Amy	724	Haverty, Bob
870	Garcia, Vidal	467	Haynes, I. D.
391	Garner, Paul	1139	Hays, Ed
290	Gayler, Manerd	422	Hazen, Jimmie
		71	Heacock, Steve

1727	Hebert, Clyde	361	Jorgenson, Ivan
124	Hefner, Hoytt	1085	Kane, Bill
879	Henry, Carol D.	33	Kenny, James
1328	Henson, Claude	1342	Knight, Faye
401	Henson, Heavy	37	Knight, Harry
667	Hill, Clayton	102	Knight, Nick
1832	Hill, Clinton	1607	Knapp, Jack
856	Hill, Jess	1069	Lamar, Curtis
1708	Hill, Jim	1848	La Rue, Walt
184	Hill, Lawrence	2051	Lawrence, Billy
501	Hines, Dan	1186	Laycock, Jim
1090	Hinkle, George	688	Laycock, Maurice
278	Hinton, Dee	1947	Leach, Billy
331	Hock, John	1873	Lee, Clarence
1392	Hoffman, Don	453	Lee, Cotton
75	Hogan, Tom	770	Lefton, Abe
1390	Holcomb, Elmer	225	Legett, Elton
233	Holder, A. J.	799	Lewallen, G. K.
411	Homoki, Stephen Cook	568	Lichtenstein, Helen
1105	Hood, Charley	1756	Lilley, H. L.
1107	Hood, Lesley	22	Linder, Herman
728	Horner, Mildred Mix	349	Lindsey, John
385	Hovencamp, Eddie	288	Lindues, Louis
387	Howard, Bill	1471	Lisenbee, Byron
1082	Howe, Don	155	Logue, Harry
188	Hubbard, Fay	1579	Lohr, Art
443	Hubbell, Rube	1840	Lorimer, Chuck
376	Hudson, Jim	77	Lovelady, Fannye
416	Hull, Mark	1999	Lovelady, Sam
1420	Hunter, Maynard	1124	Lowry, Bill
881	Hussey, Shirley	479	Lucas, Mitze
171	Hutchinson, Lee	601	Lucas, Tad
417	Hydson, Shorty	2010	Lufkin, Ned
957	Iler, Bill	1532	Lynch, Emmet
163	Iler, Mary	1646	Maggini, Charlie
176	Irwin, Jim	1900	Malm, Ted
160	Ivory, Perry	1953	Molone, Buddy
1751	Ivory, Raymond	1927	Mann, Orval
86	Jacobs, Slats	1468	Mansfield, Bob
1466	Jamison, B. M. Jr.	237	Mansfield, Toots
284	Jaques, Joseph	445	Markeum, Wolf
32	Jauregui, Andy	79	Marsh, Earl
486	Jauregui, Ed	632	Marshall, Grant
1685	Jenkins, Jay	1979	Marshall Kermit
472	Jesperson, Allen	189	Martin, Johnny

1158	Matlock, Shorty	268	McLaughlin, Donald
511	Meeks, Al	277	McLaughlin, Gene
1055	Meeks, Bob	1983	McLennon, Don
664	Mendes, Joe	1984	McLennon, Hope
208	Mendes, John	563	McMacken, Bill
111	Merchant, Richard	1936	McMahon, Ed.
107	Merritt, King	706	McWiggins, Zack
109	Meyers, Herbert	282	Neal, Bill Jr.
228	Miller, Bob	1875	Neal, Buddy
244	Miller, Richard	1678	Nelson, George W.
220	Mills, Geo.	31	Nesbitt, Donald
222	Mills, Hank	158	Nichols, J. D.
354	Minor, Kenneth	105	Nix, Will
62	Moe, Milt	317	Nolan, Bob
1386	Montana, Louise	798	Nuckols, Grafton
1385	Montana, Montie	1306	Oakey, Russell Jack
1955	Montana's Troupe	47	O'Callahan, Fox
1251	Montana, Montie, Jr.	397	Ohrlin, Glenn
1601	Montgomery, Vic	1138	Oja, Andy
1888	Moore, Bob	484	O'Shea, Michael
26	Moore, Earl	297	Overson, Bob
1196	Moore, Ward	296	Overson, Don
1746	Morris, Claude	98	Owens, Del
842	Morris, Peewee	179	Owens, Mitchell
1649	Moss, Hoitt	60	Pardee, E.
494	Mounce, Louis	53	Parker, Bud
209	Mueller, H. H.	390	Parks, Bill
93	Mulkey, Burell	552	Parks, Darwin
1934	Murphy, Hardy	994	Parrish, Vester
2024	Murray, Joe, Jr.	420	Paul, Chuck
6	Murray, Leo	2015	Payne, Gene H.
1612	McBride, Bill	473	Pearce, Joe
1737	McCarroll, Frank	460	Percifield, Jack
84	McCarty, Ed	505	Perkins, Len
1881	McCormick, Trixie	154	Peters, Floyd
20	McCrorey, Howard	320	Peterson, Buck
353	McCrorey, Shorty	880	Pettcock, U. A.
822	McDaniel, Bud	27	Pettigrew, Homer
243	McEntire, John	1822	Pettit, Japson
1149	McFadden, Gordon	1084	Pettit, Wesley
307	McFarland, Bill	788	Phillips, Dub
846	McFarland, John	504	Pholson, Jim
2	McGinty, Rusty	161	Pickett, Joseph W.
776	McGuire, Bill	398	Piela, Jack
1602	McKitrick, Walt	92	Piela, Joe

153

293	Pittman, Paul	436	Russell, S. G.
1151	Poage, Doug	256	Ryan, Duward
1143	Poage, Walton	407	Ryon, Don, Jr.
468	Pogue, John	116	Salinas, Juan
114	Powers, Ted	466	Salinas, Tony
1286	Preston, C. P.	671	Salisbury, Jack
300	Pretti, Bob	66	Saunders, Jack
690	Pruett, Gene	1101	Saunders, Jim R.
1806	Pruitt, I. V.	42	Schell, Asbury
1032	Rambo, Gene	1783	Schmidt, Doc
221	Randall, Glen H.	186	Schneide, Frankie
1818	Reeves, Jimmie	1993	Schrade, Jack
796	Reeves, Lem	1491	Schumacher, Jim
1637	Reger, Monty	330	Schwartz, Jack
1815	Reid, Nig	81	Schwarz, Vic
216	Reynolds, Brown Jug	932	Scott, Bob
196	Reynolds, Fess	931	Scott, Paul
56	Rhodes, John	1965	Seales, Kenney
46	Rhodes, Tom	1982	Selby, Bill
598	Rider, Pauline	100	Sellers, Earl
	(Mrs. Miles)	73	Sellers, Jack
1489	Ridley, Howard	723	Sells, Albert
305	Ridley, Hugh	234	Sewalt, Royce
1962	Rife, Syl	2020	Seward, Roy S.
1899	Riggs, Murray	7	Shaw, Everett
575	Roane, Sylvester	217	Shaw, Glen
175	Robbins, Dick	180	Sheppard, Chuck
1810	Roberson, A. A.	439	Sherman, Jack
651	Roberts, Geo. (Kid)	1963	Shessler, Solly
720	Roberts, Gerald	847	Shields, Chas. A.
259	Roberts, Ken	1893	Shoulders, Marvin
491	Roberts, Marjorie	1182	Shultz, Chas.
103	Roberts, Rube	260	Sievers, Bill
714	Robertson, Jim	1203	Sikes, L. N.
1658	Robinson, Buck	426	Silvers, Joe S.
1437	Rogers, Bedell	1596	Siminoff, yale
912	Rogers, Eddie	1692	Simms, Olan
1195	Rooke, Frank	165	Skelton, Al
1092	Rose, Parry	1643	Skinner, Ray
474	Rothel, Bob	1935	Slim, Colorado
1932	Rowe, Floyd	754	Sloan, Jimmie
462	Ruckdeschel, Hank	1985	Smith, Jute
57	Rude, Ike	1641	Smith, M. L.
1461	Rumsey, Jack	1855	Smith, Neal
475	Russell, Phillip	197	Smith, Roy

40	Snyder, Smoky	1707	Walker, Ike
1868	Sonnenberg, Virginia	2002	Walker, George
61	Sorrels, Buckshot	135	Ward, Bill
249	Spealman, Bud	464	Ward, Jack
310	Spencer, Tim	400	Ward, James P.
549	Spilsbury Bud	985	Ware, Slick
369	Springer, Bennie	1530	Watts, bill
1961	Squires, Wally	1930	Webster, Shote
469	Standefer, Buck	681	Wening, Richard
337	Starr, Hans	139	Westfall, Howard
1343	St. Croy, Paul	345	Whaley, Slim
1225	Stensen, Joe	1977	Whatley, Todd
351	Steward, Whitey	1820	Whetsel, Joe
1477	Stroud, Francis	1123	White, Homer
193	Stuart, Roy	1552	White, Jim
1120	Stuckey, Tom	1269	White, Sam
510	Swarts, Clem	617	White, Vivian
579	Tacker, Ike	128	Whiteman, Jim
1299	Tacquard, Kidd	214	Whorton, Al
1224	Talbot, Joe	213	Whorton, Eddie
334	Targerson, Bill	424	Wicker, Olds
336	Targerson, Slim	363	Wier, Clyde
1823	Taylor, Dan	817	Wilcox, Don
88	Teague, George	134	Wilderspin, Geo.
421	Teague, Joe	1812	Wilkens, Lefty
36	Thode, Earl	752	Williams, Ken
757	Thomas, Orville	218	Williams, Pete
1860	Thomas, Park	198	Williams, R. W.
1842	Thomas, Ray	333	Wills, Arnie
1549	Thompson, Ralph	1726	Wofford, Earl
313	Tiffin, Buck	2013	Wood, Joe
1235	Truan, Norma Holmes	677	Wood, Tom
		1877	Wright, Cecil
5	Truitt, Dick	1964	Wulfekuhler, L. W.
1903	Truman, Floyd (Sonny)	516	Yardley, George
		1100	Yates, Fayette
328	Tubbs, John	1013	York, S. A.
51	Turk, Charlie	264	Youchum, Ted
849	Tyler, Glenn	1776	Young, Paul
497	Vance, Johnnie	451	Young, Weldon
509	Vassar, Everett		
327	Van Meter, Frank		
1797	Volz, John		
191	Wade, Joe H.		
1905	Wadsworth, Glen		

DECEASED MEMBERS OF CTA

Number	Name	Number	Name
43	Barkdoll, Lee	612	Hunter, Dummy
1585	Bogan, Bill	1800	Jordon, Lon
725	Brannon, Rose	1402	Knight, Jack
877	Burkitt, Buck	78	Knight, Pete
1012	Burroughs, Wayne	1	Nesbitt, Jimmie
482	Conners, Beverly	1805	Nunn, John
1284	Couch, Worth N.	142	McClure, Jake
453	Daniels, George	844	Paxton, Trent
H5	Dew, Frank Y.	H30	Penrose, Spencer
1561	Dillon, Jack	319	Sandall, Hubert
553	Doyle, Tex	986	Stober, Earl
242	Ferris, Lee	95	Strickland, Hugh
H65	Gelvin, Floyd	1228	Welch, Slim
682	Grey, Reva	252	Wilkinson, Johnnie
41	Hill, Shorty	873	Wood, Opal

CTA MEMBERS SERVING IN THE ARMED FORCES OF OUR COUNTRY

Number	Name	Number	Name
1712	Albin, J. D.	703	Burk, Dee
298	Allen, Lonnie	1261	Burleigh, B. E. (Bryan)
1019	Arnold, Edward		
1920	Arnold, Edward	59	Burrell, Joe
1475	Atkinson, Almus	442	Cameron, Eddie
1962	Autry, Gene	55	Carr, Clay
493	Barker, Dick	261	Chambers, Bob
1202	Barron, N. E.	1732	Chapas, Max
1758	Barton, Bill	1443	Chipman, John
1391	Becker, Johnny	1839	Coffey, Ed
795	Beken, Henry	406	Colbert, Charles
1495	Bell, Melvin	1152	Cole, Chili
236	Bennett, Charlie	2014	Coe, H. A.
969	Black, Billy	887	Colbert, Dude (Chas.)
819	Blackstone, Doc		
83	Blevins, Earl	1719	Crawford, Bill
1959	Bohlender, Ike	1576	Crossland, Leo
833	Booth, Leslie	1247	Darnel, Clarence
1784	Boss, Ray	1824	Davis, Arthur
1353	Boyer, Bob	230	Davis, Buck
1925	Boyhan, John H.	2012	Dillon, Ben
1097	Brannon, Leo	629	Duarte, Hoot

Number	Name	Number	Name
67	McEuen, Albert	525	Talbot, Jim
1634	McEuen, Arthur	1844	Teague, Earl
1591	McDougle, Buck	1931	Thode, Henry
39	McGee, Jimmie	49	Truan, Fritz
1748	McLaughlin, James	961	Valdez, Shorty
	(Spec.)	1580	Vinas, Joe
755	Nelson, Tim	777	Vincent, Marion
1444	Oldenberg, John	211	Wagner, Neil
1575	Oliver, Buck	1397	Wallace, James A.
52	Owsley, Cecil	254	Walls, Elmo
1916	Padgett, Ray	126	Watkins, Ward
1542	Palmer, Johnny	965	Westinghouse, Buddy
389	Parker, Rock	1785	Whatley, Cliff
322	Patch, Jim	566	Whitaker, Vern
1387	Pattee, Alan	794	White, Woodrow
324	Paul, Marvin		Whiteman, Hub
1849	Pogue, John	650	Whiting, Bob
1799	Porter, Jack C.	1248	Wilkins, Don
235	Pribble, M.O. (Mike)	1533	Witty, R. L.
441	Quirk, Frank	1551	Williams, Carl
2021	Roger, Buddy	1725	Williams, Jake
1376	Ribelin, Tom	1465	Williams, Lee Roy
2014	Richardson, Lloyd	1490	Woods, Charlie
1890	Ritches, Bob	1645	Wright, Jim
1335	Robinson, Lucky	359	Yonnick, Buttons
1341	Rooker, Bob		
589	Ross, Bruce		
1874	Rogers, Pete		
1219	Servel, Pierre		
1662	Shannon, L. V.		
348	Shellenberger, C.J.		
936	Shellenberger, D.C.		
2011	Sisco, Jack		
1694	Snure, Ben		
1831	Spruel, Johnny		
1776	Stockdale, Champie		
38	Stout, David		
1946	Stoval, John		
1656	Swenson, Allen		
19	Stanton, Ralph		
1496	Swartout, George		
1693	Taylor, Ed		
1401	Taylor, Hubert, Jr.		

Number	Name	Number	Name
1959	Durham, John	1578	Jerrel, Jerry
1010	Dwyer, Emmett	299	Jones, Cecil
1642	Dyer, Paul	1915	Kaaro, Jimmy
1721	Emery, Harold	1393	Kelley, Billy
296	Emory, Harold	1892	Kelley, Bob
169	Engelsman, Led	1308	Kelley, Jack
1525	Ensley, Allen	1394	Kelley, Truman
596	Eskew, Junior	295	Kerscher, Pete
1234	Eskew, Tom Mix	878	Killough, Buck
1616	Evans, Johnnie	294	Knight, Tom
859	Fancher, Ben	843	Klebba, Joe
1918	Felton, Boots	18	Koed, Whitely
1795	Fennack, Tony	489	Kohrs, Ray
203	Ferrario, Amil	670	Kudron, Ray
1869	Fetters, Bob	1608	Kumerle, Slim
1273	Fife, Harold	1221	Lane, Ralph
402	Finley, Frank	1569	Lasswell, Chuck
396	Finley, Luther	1414	Lawrence, Junior
1329	Fisher, Bud	683	Like, James
291	Fisher, Mike	1570	Linderman, Bud
17	Fleming, Joel	857	Londos, Swede
653	Fletcher, Al	1215	Lovelady, Shorty
87	Fletcher, Kid	1906	Luer, Harvey
1990	Forsyth, Rollin	1025	Lyon, Stan
1527	Fox, Dewey	1900	Malm, Ted
7	Goodspeed, Red	1426	Maddox, Everett
45	Gordon, Alvin	364	Marion, Frank
1796	Gregory, Bern	382	Matthews, Bob
1483	Guy, Eddie	866	Mefford, Bud
1216	Haas, Chuck	697	Melville, Bob
1005	Hamilton, Eugene	1031	Mendes, Carl
28	Hancock, Sonny	1030	Mendes, Frank
753	Harriss, Baylis	1749	Merritt, Denn
1958	Haynes, Thos. D.	1896	Merritt, Hyde
183	Henley, Cecil	1661	Miles, Dave
933	Herren, Dick	1447	Miller, George
1117	Hickman, Chester	1633	Mott, Eddie
876	Hightower, William C.	666	Mounce, Ernest
1650	Hillyer, Jack	1829	Munson, Bryan
1937	Hoggett, Chas.	1289	Mutch, Ernest
1404	Holleyman, J. D.	1902	McBride, Dudley
1360	Howell, Chet	1450	McCabe, Tommy
1958	Hurd, Lee R.	1113	McCormick, J. D.

HONORARY MEMBERS OF CTA

Number	Name	Number	Name
123	Abbey, Chariman	48	Faubion, W. L.
107	Aber, Lynn	79	Faulk, Hamilton
82	Addington, John E.	9	Fisher, Ham
105	Agee, John	127	Forest, R. W.
32	Allred, Gov. James	286	Francisco, Bill
33	Ammons, Teller	292	Freyer, Dick
64	Baird, Dr. Vernon	72	Frock, Eldon
307	Barnes, H. M.	71	Fuentez, Juan
308	Bell, John H.	119	Fugitt, Jack
99	Bell, W. M.	275	Gibson, John L.
255	Ben, Rodeo Tailor	35	Godshall, Jeane
15	Black Foot Elks	102	Goode, Jim
	Lodge	100	Govier, H. R.
128	Bonelli, William G.	43	Haines, Willard
4	Booth, Tom	25	Hamberger, Phil
129	Booth, W. H.	58	Harris, Helen M.
296	Brady, Kathleen	289	Harris, Robert S.
295	Brady, Dr. Leo	276	Hartman, Genl.
305	Brink, M.E. "Bob"	37	Hatfield, George
81	Brown, Arthur	38	Hines, Cherry Hale
56	Buchanan, R. B.	294	Hofmann, R. J.
93	Butterfield, Chas.	76	Hopkins, Ma
28	Call, Grant	77	Hopkins, Pa
108	Carr, Bill	12	Hopp, Pete
74	Conklin, Roy	22	Howe, J. C. (Red)
300	Cooper, Tex	307	Hughes, Chas. J.
8	Coze, Paul	36	Hughes, Joe D.
34	Cullington, Geo.	272	Hutchins, Barbara K.
114	Cummings, Harrie B.	14	Jernigan, Buck
301	Davis, Lillian	98	John V. M.
66	Deglin, Ted	39	Johnson, E. H.
110	Dickson, Dick	57	Johnson, Everett
54	Dillon, Roy M.	40	Johnson, Mervin L.
138	Doheny, Tim	61	Jones, R.T. (Bob)
63	Dudley, Dorris	73	Justin, H.J. & Sons
50	Dunckon, Fred	137	Kellenberger, A.G.
17	Dunn, P.C.	10	Kilpatrick, Col. John
303	Echols, Ed.		Reed
291	Elliott, Bill	101	Kimmel, H.R.
109	Evans, Bill	21	Kriendler, Jack
280	Falk, Ace	299	Kriz, Joe

159

Number	Name	Number	Name
1	La Farge, Wanden	41	Rich, Cap
69	Lahman, Jerry	103	Riley, Frank
96	Lane, Casper	7	Riling, Raymond
	"Cappy"	290	Robison, Beanie
288	Lee, Albert	283	Rogers, Roy
45	Lee, W. A.	122	Root, Helene
293	Leonard, R. J.	120	Root, Lloyd L.
51	Lewis, H. G.	121	Root, Louise
89	Lewis, K. W.	999	Ross, Butch
104	Lockhard, Sonny	297	Rowett, Wm.
68	Lovejoy, Eiland	620	Ryley, Frank
273	McDowell, Paul	88	Sandefer, G. B.
281	McCumber, W. R.	86	Sands, George
46	McClure, Marion B.	23	Sartwelle, J. W.
	McEuen, Ed.	67	Saunders, R. L.
84	Majors, Cliff	62	Sawyers, Ed.
502	Manning, Art	87	Sawyers, Pauline
116	Mansfield, Monte, Jr.	47	Schooley, Herschel
80	Martens, Jack	130	Scoma, Joe
3	Martin, Prosser	131	Scully, J. M.
85	Massey, Gus	271	Searls, R. D.
125	Mason, Fred L.	135	Shepherd, V. H.
27	Mathews, E. R.	111	Sherman, Harry
112	Meigs, Henry	646	Shinn, Chas. A.
3	Michelson, Dr.	278	Smith, Governor
	Henry E.	302	Sommers, Gerald E.
126	Miller, Arthur C.	16	Steelman, Hosea E.
29	Miller, Dan	11	Steward, Mrs.
95	Moore, Frank		Jacqueline A.
134	Motschall, Katherine	24	Strake, Geo. W.
136	Murrells, Dan T.	49	Talbott, Ray H.
304	Newell, Pauline B.	118	Templeton, M. L.
117	Newell, Walter L.	75	Thomas, Pat
83	Newhagen, Frank E.	44	Travelier, Gil
300	O'Brien, Eddie	292	Tunis, John W.
59	Oltorf, Jack G.	115	Turk, Dad
60	Oltorf, Mrs. Jack G.	306	Tyrell, Ace
18	Parker, Gus	20	Tussing L. Benton
19	Paul, Clyde	281	Ungerer, Ray
42	Perkins, Arthur	284	Ward, Fay
13	Potter, Lyle Van	279	Warden, General
139	Porter, Pat	92	Warren, W. B.
2	Randolph, Floyd	31	Watson, Bill
		277	Webb, Mg. J. R.

Number	Name
53	Wheelis, Penn
106	White, Edwin R.
6	Whiteman, Paul
274	Williams, Thomas O.
78	Witham, Wayne
55	Wolf, Ralph R.
91	Wrigley, Phillip K.
90	Yoder, Phil

Authors Note:

What a trip down "memory lane," this Turtle Rule Book has been for me! I hadn't thought of some of these fellas listed in the roster for some fifty years. To see all these names in print brought back many fond reflections. I didn't know all of these people personally, but it surprised me just how many stories I could relate about so very many of them. Guess this book could go on for a long time, but...

Most of these men are gone now, but certainly not forgotten. I hope those of you who are still with us will get as much pleasure from this look back into some real sports history, as I have.

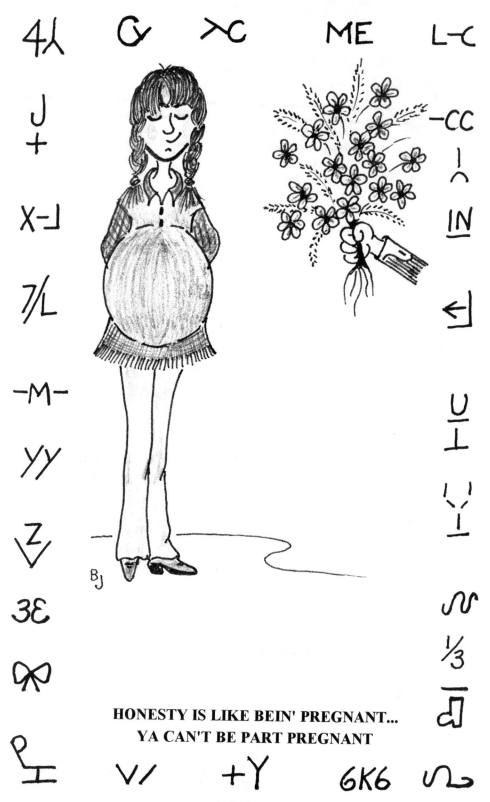

**HONESTY IS LIKE BEIN' PREGNANT...
YA CAN'T BE PART PREGNANT**

Horses

_⊥✗ '95_

IT'S EASY TO RIDE A GOOD HORSE TO DEATH...
THE SAME APPLIES TO A NEIGHBOR

THE PERSON THAT DOESN'T LOVE A HORSE
HAS MISSED A LOT OF LIVIN'

Anne Stradling of Patagonia, Arizona, with her team of greys, Barney and Clyde, in 1984. Anne is honored in the Cowgirl Hall of Fame in Hereford, Texas.

S^H

THE WAY TO A COWBOY'S HEART IS
THROUGH HIS HORSE

Everett Bowman, winner of the calf roping at the Cheyenne Frontier Days Rodeo in 1927. His average time on three calves from a sixty-foot *SCORE* was 21.4 seconds. Through his career Everett used several celebrated horses: Mickey, Coon Dog, Chino, Possum, Speckle Back, and a few more.

DON'T EXPECT APPLAUSE... DESERVE IT

THE WAY TO A COWGIRL'S HEART
IS THROUGH HER HORSE

Margie Greenough Henson at Madison Square Garden
Rodeo in New York City, N.Y. in 1938.

"BACK UP PETE"

Among his many rodeo wins in the 1920's and 30's, probably one of the more prestigious to Ed Bowman (and his famous horse Pete) was the All-Around Championship at the Prescott, Arizona rodeo in 1927. Here, at age of forty-one, while most of his competitors were ten years or more his junior, he was awarded the Hoot Gibson Trophy for tying three calves on a sixty-foot *SCORE* in an average of 18.3 seconds. That record was never broken until the calf roping score was shortened to thirty feet and ultimately to what the short scores of today are.

Ed Bowman and "Back Up Pete" at home with the Hoot Gibson Trophy won at Prescott, Arizona in 1927.

WHEN YA HAVE A HORSE WITH A HEART AS BIG AS A WASH TUB, FEED HIM HIS OATS FROM YOUR HAND

Ed's Hoot Gibson Trophy, or as Ed corrrected, Pete's trophy was donated to the Cowboy Hall of Fame in Oklahoma City, Oklahoma where Ed is honored alongside his brother Everett.

IT PAYS TO HAVE A LEAN HORSE FOR A LONG RACE

Ed Bowman, first rider out at the second change of horses in the *STRAP AND CINCH RELAY RACE* at the Prescott, Arizona Frontier Days Rodeo in 1927.

One of the keys to Uncle Ed's success in his nine-year reign of this event was his acute ability and judgment concerning a horse. He was always on the lookout for good running horses for this race and for his rope horses. Back Up Pete and Gringo were his two main mounts through his nine years of racing; he acquired both from the thorough-bred race track strings of Breezy and Otho Cox of Duncan, Arizona. Gringo was a stallion who sired many fine colts that developed into top rope and cow horses for Ed. The story has been told about the exceptional, Back Up Pete.

ALWAYS SUPPORT THE WEIGHT OF YOUR OWN SHOULDERS

Ed Bowman and Cap in 1947. Cap was another "Back Up Pete," one of many fine cow horses that Ed raised by his stallion, Gringo. During practice, Ed and Cap roped calves by the hour without Cap wearing a bridle.

AN HONEST HORSE IS LIKE A GOOD NEIGHBOR... ALWAYS THERE....

Pal, another great offspring of Gringo, raised by Ed Bowman at the Hook and Line in the early 1940's. Pal weighed over twelve hundred pounds and made a *WHALE* of a *STEER HORSE*.

THE BEST VIEW YA EVER GET OF A WINNER IS HIS HIP POCKETS

THESE LEGS WERE MADE FOR RIDIN'

Ed Bowman at age sixty-six, waiting at the front door of his "Motel" for his turn up in the *CUTTING* contest with Sonny Boy in 1952.

**WHEN YOU ARE STANDIN' TALL IN THE
SADDLE, KEEP PUSHIN' HARD ON YOUR
STIRRUPS SO YOU WILL BE SURE TO
STAY THERE**

Ed Bowman and Sonny Boy at a *CUTTING* contest in
1952.

Sonny Boy's only fault in the first stages of his training as
a *CUTTING* horse was his tendency to get too close to the

174

animal he was herding... he wanted to bite 'em! Credits to the contestant's score were discounted in *CUTTING* competition if the rider pulled on the bridle reins, so Ed taught Sonny Boy to "get back" with a nudge of the *SPURS*.

Uncle Ed Bowman never completely retired from professional rodeo competition. At the age of fifty-five, after training many more "Back Up Petes," he curtailed his serious roping competition and at the age of sixty-four, took up professional cutting horse competition. He moved from his Hook and Line Ranch of forty years to his ranch near Peyton, Colorado. Here he set about intensely training Sonny Boy, his cutting horse for professional competition.

He was soon in the winners circle of cutting horse contests and at the age of sixty-seven, he and Sonny Boy won the Anerican Quarter Horse Association Cutting Contest. Together in one year, they won the Western States, Pacific Coast and National Cutting Horse Association's titles. Many of his younger competitors made the mistake of trying to out ride the "old man" in the arena, but Ed's summation of his success was, "Sonny Boy could cut the soda out of a biscuit."

Hugh Bennett, a noted breeder and judge of the American Quarter Horse, once told me, "When both Ed and Sonny Boy are at their best they're unbeatable." (Hugh is honored in the American Quarter Horse Hall of Fame, National Cowboy Hall of Fame and Pro Rodeo Hall of Fame.)

WHEN YA GOT IT... YA GOT IT!....

Ed Bowman at the celebration of his win of the
American Quarter Horse Association contest on his
CUTTING horse, Sonny Boy in 1953.

COWBOYS APPEAR TO BE *ROUGH UNDER THE
COLLAR...* **BUT THEY ARE MOSTLY QUITE
CARING....**

LAUGHTER IS THE GREATEST OF THERAPIES

RIDIN' A GOOD WORKIN' HORSE IS LIKE EATIN' A GOOD MEAL... IT MAKES YER BODY HAPPY

Ed Bowman
Peyton, Colorado, 1952

Black Powder being trained in *THE SCHOOL OF HARD KNOCKS* as a back-up cuttin' horse for Sonny Boy. This "no-nonsense" horse was a "powerhouse." He was never entered in competition, but had that natural instinct and drive to be a champion.

Skeet Bowman and Patsy, one of his ranch raised fillies, in 1950. Patsy won blue ribbons in halter show horse classes. She was entered in the Ruidoso Quarter Horse Racing Futurity in New Mexico, and went on to become a successful race horse.

CONTENTMENT FOR A COWBOY IS SADDLIN' A GOOD HORSE

Skeet Bowman on Poco Miss, one of the last fine horses he raised. At age seventy-eight, Skeet is waiting for his turn in a performance class. Skeet became noted for the good "Paints" he raised in the 1970's, accumulating a room full of trophies they won in halter and performance classes.

SURE WISH WE COULD GET *REINFORCEMENT OF VOCAL SOUNDS BY SYMPATHETIC VIBRATION* BACK INTO OUR WESTERN MUSIC

Rex Allen, Morton Bodfish, Everett Bowman, Ed Bowman at the Desert Caballeros Ride at Wickenburg, Arizona, in 1950.

TIME FLIES WHEN YER HAVIN' FUN....

IT'S NOT WHAT YA KNOW... IT'S WHO YA KNOW

Mules

WELL LITTLE FELLER, I GOT'EM SHOD... THAT NEW HAND IS SO LAZY HE WOULDN'T HOLLER SUEY IF THE HOGS WERE EATIN' HIM....

WHEN YA *PACK A MULE*....USE A *DIAMOND HITCH* SO NOTHIN' WILL *RATTLE AROUND*

"Hawk Canyon Transfer Company" in 1919.

⟨8⟩

Ed Bowman at the Hook and Line Ranch as a *REP* from his Steeple Eight Ranch, six miles up the creek.

Uncle Ed, at the age of twenty-nine, moved from the San Francisco River country above Clifton, Arizona in 1915, and established his Steeple Eight Ranch in Hawk Canyon. George Graham, his father-in-law, had bought the Hook and Line Ranch, six miles below the present Coolidge Dam, from W. O. Tutle. He *STAKED* Ed to fifty head of wild cows and enough range land to run them in order to secure good help, thus giving Ed his start as a ranch owner.

NEVER WALK UP BEHIND A MULE UNLESS YOU ARE TIRED OF THE LIFE STYLE YOU ARE LIVING

Ed Bowman and George Graham with the "Sure Freight"
division of the Hook and Line Ranch about 1920.

Looks like Uncle Ed has loaded everything but the
"kitchen sink" on the two mules. But then, a closer inspec-
tion of the *PACKS* indicates that he might have included
that too!

I remember when I was about ten years old, Uncle Ed
had one exceptionally ornery mule named Sugar. The name
certainly didn't fit her dispostion so I asked, "Why such a
sweet name for a such a sour mule?" Uncle Ed answered,

"When Sugar was young I used her in the pack string to Rupkey's store at San Carlos. She was more ornery than most from the start and I hadn't come up with a disgusting enough name that would fit her.

On one of those trips I loaded one hundred pounds of flour on one side of her and one hundred pounds of sugar on the other side. I usually *PACKED* five to seven or eight mules at Rupkey's. When I started home, I tied the lead ropes up to their necks and turned them loose, then followed behind them. Naturally they wanted to go home so it was easier and faster for them to travel, unhindered from being tied in a line.

'Bout halfway home this day, Sugar was doing her damndest to be miserable. She ran under a mesquite tree that had low, dead limbs, and one of them poked a big hole in the bottom of the sack of sugar and turned the *PACK*. Before I could rope her and stop the wreck, most of the sugar had leaked out on the ground. Quite an expensive loss in those days! From then on this 'darling' little mule became known as 'Sugar'."

**WHEN YA GOT ONE ALWAYS JUMPIN'
THE FENCE, IT MIGHT BE A GOOD IDEA
TO HUNT UP YER *HOBBLES***

MOTIVATING A MULE IS LIKE TRYIN' TO GET BLOOD OUT OF A TURNIP

Lois Bowman, wife of Everett, punchin' cows on their Five Cross Ranch, west of Safford, Arizona, in 1933.

Like all ranch wives, Aunt Lois could make a *HAND* at anything that had to be done on the ranch. Aside from being a great cowpuncher, she was a *WHALE* of a cook, housekeeper, "chore boy", navigator on the rodeo trail, and a great mother to me in my travels with her and Uncle Everett. She was my pal. Many of the quips in this book came from her; she was a genius at it.... a great humorist.

WHEN YA WANT SOMETHIN' DONE, GO DO IT

WHO SAID THERE AIN'T NO SUCH THING AS A GOOD MULE?

Dick Bowman on Sally at brother Ed's, Hook and Line Ranch in 1946.

Uncle Ed bought Sally from Fred Upshaw, our neighboring rancher to the south. It was a five-hour trail ride to Fred's place over steep, rocky country. I took delivery on Sally at Fred's about noon, saddled her up and started for home. She was *GREEN* broke and didn't know much. I'll never forget that trip home! It took more like seven hours but she was much tamer on arrival.

A SPOILED MULE CAN BE HAZARDOUS TO YOUR HEALTH

John Ortega with the Hook and Line "construction
company" in 1947.

When John came to work for me at the age of sixteen in
1946, he could do anything on a cow ranch that any experienced cowboy could do. It didn't matter what kind of the
various ranch jobs was at hand, he always produced a little
more than the man working next to him. His father, Dutch
Ortega, a noted top cowman in the Globe, Arizona area,
trained his many children to excel. It's not surprising that
John became, and still is, the "Head Man" of one of the
largest cow ranches in Gila County, Arizona, the H and E
Ranch.

TOO MANY 14 AND 16 HOUR DAYS ON THE JOB CAN *HANG YA OUT TO DRY*

John Ortega and I cleaned out the Bull Basin tank in 1948 with the "Hook and Line Bulldozer." Blondie, in the middle of the *HITCH,* is one of the *BRONC* mules from the *REMUDA.*

We packed anything, sometimes just sand, but usually feed and water for the teams on two to four bronc mules each morning. We worked these broncs in the team all day, then rode them home. After such a day's work, these spirited animals were somewhat docile. Six weeks of this procedure and our broncs were pretty well on the road to being broke.

PACKIN' A BRONC MULE **IS LIKE DOIN' BUSINESS WITH AN OPPOSING LAWYER... YA BETTER** *TIE A FOOT UP....*

Spence and Minnie under full *PACK* enroute to the Poverty Flat Tank on the Hook and Line in December, 1949. Had to tie one of Minnie's hind feet up to her neck to get her loaded.

PACKIN' A BRONC MULE **AT DAY LIGHT IN DECEMBER CAN** *TEST YER AIR....*

SADDLIN' A BRONC MULE AT DAYLIGHT IN DECEMBER CAN *WIND YER CLOCK*

FRECKLES, in *THE SCHOOL OF HARD KNOCKS*

All of my uncles, Ed, Everett, Walt, and Skeet were good *HANDS* at breaking mules. They must have inherited the ability from their father, who was a master. The process, somewhat different from breaking horses, wasn't a natural one for me, but I learned some of the "tricks" from the uncles.

One time I asked Uncle Ed what he considered to be the greatest single item in mule breaking. His reply was, "Just keep jerkin' the wet saddle blankets off of him, and watch out that he doesn't kick ya in the belly five years after you've called him broke!"

THE GREATEST SINGLE ITEM YOU CAN USE IN
BREAKING A MULE IS WET SADDLE BLANKETS

John "Hot Shot" Cox, son of Breezy Cox, and Ed
Bowman working the Hook and Line "Construction
Company."

Uncle Ed was a genius at packing a mule. He packed this
huge plow all over the sixty section, Hook and Line Ranch.
The monstrosity weighed about two hundred pounds. There
was no way that I could keep the danged thing loaded on a
mule until I dismantled the long cumbersome tongue, and
then I still had pure Hell!

WHEN YA GET A GOOD *SCALD* ON A SITUATION..
DON'T TRY TO IMPROVE ON IT...

WHEN YOU HAVE THE TOUCH OF A BLACKSMITH... DON'T TRY TO BE A WATCHMAKER....

"Hot Shot" was quite a hand. When he wasn't workin' the "construction company," he was gettin' a good start in the horseshoein' business.

SOME COWBOYS YOU HIRE ARE DANDIES TO TAKE WITH YA, BUT YA SURE CAN'T SEND THEM

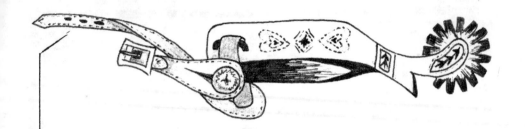

BREAKIN' A *STRING OF MULES* CAN MAKE YA
MEANER THAN A JUNK YARD DOG

NEVER APPROACH A MULE FROM THE REAR,
A BULL FROM THE FRONT, OR A CROOK
FROM ANY DIRECTION

WHEN THE BOSS CUTS THE "HAS BEENS" AND
"WILL BE'S" FOR YER MOUNTS, IT MIGHT PAY
TO ASK HIM IF HE'S GOT ANY "IS NOW'S"

MOST *MULE HEADED* MEN HAVE THEIR HEAD
UP THEIR ASS

BREAKIN' TWELVE *BRONC* MULES IN
ONE SETTIN' CAN *YANK YER CHAIN*

Dogs

**THE LOYALTY OF A DEVOTED
DOG IS COMPARABLE TO THAT
OF A GOOD WIFE AND MOTHER**

WHEN YA KNOW YOU'RE GETTIN' LOW ON BULLETS, BE SURE YER NEXT SHOT DOESN'T COME UP ON AN EMPTY CHAMBER

Everett Bowman and his father's dog, Darkus in 1916.

My grandfather Bowman and Darkus no doubt could have "made it" in the movies. Here, Everett at age seventeen, has pretended to shoot Darkus; guess the bullet just grazed him as Darkus' head is "flopped" to one side. Grandpa had an uncanny ability with all animals which he passed on to his sons. Too bad that genetic trait wasn't inherited by his grandchildren!

**MOST FOLKS (AND SOME DOGS) HAVE A
GOOD DEGREE OF INTELLIGENCE... SOME JUST
FIGGER OUT HOW TO GET MORE OUTA IT....**

Ed and Tom Bowman with Darkus in 1917.

Darkus didn't like to swim the Gila River crossings at the Hook and Line Ranch so he usually hitched a ride in this manner.

WHEN YA GET A NEW HOUND INTHE RACE,
RUN HARD WITH HIM

Grampa Bowman,
and Darkus
in 1920.

Uncle Ed was somewhat
of an animal trick trainer
also. Here he has his
horse lie flat with Darkus
in a conquering pose.

THE FIRST TWO THINGS A COW DOG NEEDS TO LEARN ARE "GET BACK" AND *"SON-OF-A-BITCH"*

Ed Bowman *CUTTING* cattle on Sonny Boy in 1950 with Happy, his Border Collie cow dog, acting as his *HOLD UP MAN*. They worked for hours on end in this manner. You can bet, both Sonny Boy and Happy knew the meaning of "Get Back". Ed taught it to Sonny Boy with his spurs, and to Happy with one sharp command.

WINNING ISN'T EVERYTHING, BUT IT SURE COMES CLOSE

MY THREE SONS

David age nineteen, Doug age seventeen, and Huey
age eight.

David became a Medical Doctor, Doug an Educator of
Handicapped Children, and Huey, a Ridge Back Hound,
became a cowdog. (He learned "get back" and
"SON-OF-BITCH" early in life.)

MOST COWBOYS HAVE THE HEART OF A
BRUTE AND THE COMPASSION OF AN ANGEL

Skeet, Everett, Ed, and Walt Bowman at the Colorado Springs Rodeo in the late 1940's, enjoying the working stock dog competition. While they never participated in this show event, all four brothers were exceptional *HANDS* at working their cowdogs on their ranches.

Many times I have witnessed Uncle Ed ride in the lead of a nervous herd of cattle and simply tell his dogs (never more than two) to "Bring 'em on." I always marveled at how seemingly easy that "crew" efficiently handled the cattle in rough, brushy country without losing an animal.

**MOST OF THE WORKIN' COW DOGS
ARE IN THE WRONG PLACE
90% OF THE TIME**

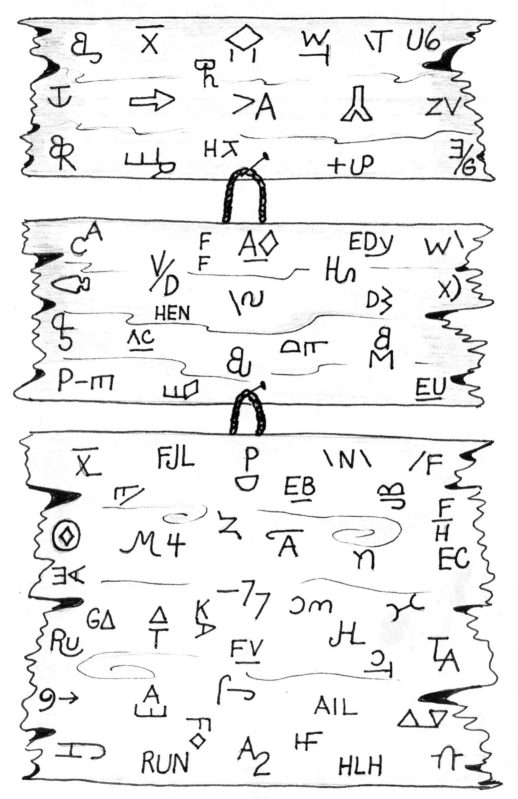

Tributes

A MAN'S HERO GETS CREDIT FOR HANGIN' THE MOON

EVERY MAN HAS A HERO

Will Rogers as he appeared at the Prescott Frontier Days Rodeo in 1933. Will made one of his *CLASSIC* speeches here during which he called himself "Saddle Bum." As history has recorded, he was much, much more. He was a cowboy first, but he went on to become a national diplomat, politician, ambassador, philosopher, writer, humorist, movie actor, and you name it. He was always a friend of the cowboy, frequenting cowboy gatherings everywhere.

This writer at age eight, had the honor of being called "friend" by Will and being taught one of his many rope tricks. He was a genius with a rope. One of his many tricks was to throw his rope out on the ground horizontally at full length, give it a flip, and when the inverted U formed in the rope in the air, he threw a half hitch over it creating a slip knot. I worked on this trick for months on end and only completed it once, giving up the task, deciding that I would never come close to Will Rogers with a rope. What a proud feller I was though in having been tutored by another of my many heroes. I have always savored my friendship as a lad with Will Rogers.

WILL ROGERS ONCE SAID HE DIDN'T KNOW MUCH ABOUT HISTORY... BUT HISTORY KNOWS ABOUT HIM

THE IMPOSSIBLE TAKES A LITTLE WHILE

W.L."Tay" Cook at age eighty-nine, bagged his last
blacktail deer.

Tay spent his entire lifetime of ninety-one years in Willcox, Arizona, the city where he was born. Truly a son of the Arizona range lands, he grew up in the business of raising and feeding cattle and horses.

In 1948, he entered politics and was elected to the House of Representatives as a spokesman for the cattlemen. He went on to serve ten terms in the "House," including three successive terms as Speaker. Tay's legislative philosophy always was, "No politics... every tub should stand on its own bottom." His definition of the difference between a politician and a statesman was that "a politican looks toward the next election, a statesman looks toward the next generation".

Tay was truly a statesman, as his record shows, and a real friend.

THE OLDER THE VIOLIN, THE SWEETER THE MUSIC

IF I'DA KNOWN I WAS GONNA LIVE THIS LONG, I'DA TOOK BETTER CARE OF MYSELF

\ ∿

SHERIFF OF COCHISE COUNTY
1965 - 1976

T.J. "Jim" Willson
1924 - 1993

-77

Jimmy and I became good friends in 1961 when we were both working for Sheriff Phil Olander of Cochise County in Eastern Arizona. Jim had been a deputy at Naco, Arizona, on the Mexican border for several years under our previous sheriff, Jack Howard when I picked up my badge of law enforcement.

Being *GREEN* at police work, I readily sought the aid of Jim, respecting his experience and the unassuming manner in which he conducted himself. Having both been cowboys all of our lives, we had a lot in common so communication, the "ultimate" on this job, was no problem.

Jimmy took me to the Mexican border, ten miles south of the county seat at Bisbee, Arizona, and started schooling me in narcotics trafficking. This matter wasn't a big problem at the time, but Jim could see the potential in what a major problem it could become and he was trying to "nip it in the bud." Had all law enforcement agencies concerning the Mexican border followed his lead at this time, narcotics "running" out of Mexico might not have reached the magnitude that it is today.

The first narcotic "stake out" that Jimmy took me on was in the middle of a cold winter night. We laid out in the brush and damn near froze to death before Jim made his move on the "bust." I never knew exactly what went wrong, but all we got out of the deal was an ol' mangy burro loaded with about thirty pounds of marijuana; the "bandits" got away. Never the less, Jimmy was overjoyed. In wonderment I asked, "What the hell are you so happy about? A helluva fine pair of cops we are, the crooks gave us the slip"! Jim replied, "Oh, we'll catch those birds another time if they come back but just look what we've got! The County is now cleaned up of dope!"

I could go on at great length with Willson stories. Some of his exploits across the border in Mexico, helping that country while helping ours, could fill a volume. In his own unique style, which I'm sure hasn't been printed in any law enforcement school books, his success as a field detective was unsurpassed. He had the complete good will and cooperation of all Mexican law enforcement agencies, a distinction which has not since been duplicated by any North American lawman. It's a pity that Jimmy's story has not been written.

In 1965 when Phil Olander retired as Sheriff of Cochise County, Jim was elected to the office. He served in that capacity until 1976 when he retired in order to assist in the organization of the Four Arizona Border Counties Strike Force, with headquarters in Tucson, Arizona, some 100 miles northwest of Bisbee. This new narcotic deterrent operation was a cooperative group of several law enforcement agencies; Jimmy's longtime dream. He was a founder and leader of the agency, still intent in his belief that narcotic trafficking on the Mexican border could be stopped. In a couple of years when the success of the organization became apparent, it evolved into the state wide, Arizona Drug Control District Strike Force with offices at the State Capitol in Phoenix. Many other states, observing the success of this unique organization, requested it's assistance in organizing their own strike force. Jim traveled to several states, lending that assistance.

Jimmy finally retired from active law enforcement work in 1984 after about thirty years of dedicated service. Many, many of us throughout Cochise County and the State of Arizona sorely miss him. He was a friend of everyone. There has never been a derogatory word heard from any source about him, and he apprehended some mighty tough crooks in his time! He was always happy, always ready to help, even if it was just to get a cat off of some older person's roof.

Jimmy was truly one of a kind. What an honor it was for me to be called "Friend" by this feller; the same has also been expressed by a multitude of others.

**SOME FELLAS MAKE THINGS HAPPEN,
OTHERS WAIT FOR THEM TO TURN UP**

WHAT A DOLL!

Cordelia Lewis of Weed, New Mexico, age ninety-six
as she is today.

\N\

Cordelia is my second cousin. She has lived in Weed
practically all of her life. She is an amazing person. With a
zest for life that few of her juniors of thirty years could

equal, she drives her new Buick car where ever she wants to go and does her own *RAT KILLIN'*.

She has been a cattle rancher, grocery store, gas station and tavern operator at Weed most of her life. She devoted a quantity of her time through her years to the care and preservation of some of the land and property passed on by her grandfather, George Lewis. She just recently retired from cattle ranching; she said she got tired of having to lead her horse up to a big rock in order to get on! She has also retired from her other life long businesses, but she continues to keep many other "irons in the fire."

I recently visited her at her home for a couple of days and I got "plum wore out" just trying to follow her! She gave me a lot of the Lewis family history that I didn't know anything about. She is a walking encyclopedia on everyone in the family tree of George and Mary Lewis who settled at Weed in 1884. There are so many Lewis descendants, there was no way in one "settin'" I could record all the history Cordelia gave me.

An annual Lewis family reunion is held at Weed in August at the old homesite of George and Mary. Cordelia is one of the "ring leaders" of the reunion and she reported that in 1994, four-hundred people attended, most of them claiming to be related! The seventh generation of the Lewis family was represented there. I surely am pleased to be related to such "stayers"; hope it's inherent!

YA DON'T SEEM AS BUSY AS SOME WHEN YA DO THINGS RIGHT THE FIRST TIME

Andrew "Shorty" Lovelady 1910 - 1994

Shorty's family located in Prescott, Arizona, in 1920, when he was ten years old. His father took care of forty-five head of the Prescott Frontier Days bucking horses, so it was only natural that Shorty followed the rodeo trail as a career.

As a small boy, Shorty worked for Doc Pardee who had a stable near the fairgrounds. Doc, who became an influential force in the development of the Prescott Frontier Days as a noted national rodeo, was the one who gave Shorty his nickname.

Shorty and his wife Fannye, purchased my uncle Everett's cow ranch near Hillside, Arizona, after they retired from professional rodeo activities in the 1940's. The two families were the best of friends and always finalized their business deals with a simple handshake which was the custom of the era.

The Loveladys and the Bowmans enjoyed many years of gratifying work together on the rodeo tour. When Everett was president of the Cowboys Turtle Association, 1936 - 1944, Fannye was the paid secretary, 1940 - 1944. This brought about an even closer bond beweeen the two couples. Aunt Lois had conducted many of the secretarial duties of the CTA since it's inception in 1936 from the back seat of the Bowman's car.

Shorty is honored in the National Cowboy Hall of Fame at Oklahoma City, and was the holder of a Gold Card from the Professional Rodeo Cowboys Association. To qualify for this card, and life-time membership, one must be fifty years old and have been a member of the PRCA for fifteen years.... Shorty was one of my pals in my younger days of rodeo travel.

R̆
O

A CATTLEMAN... A COWBOY... A GENTLEMAN

Manerd Gayler
1907 - 1990

Manerd was born in Clarmore, Oklahoma, and left home at sixteen years old after the death of his father.

He traveled to Texas where he worked as a cowboy on several ranches, and eventually followed the rodeo circuit for six or seven years. I admired this "gentleman of rodeo," and will never forget his style and manner of speech.

Manerd was a skilled roper, and made the best "catch" of his life when he married Alice Parker in 1940. Two special people came from that union, John and Francis. They, in turn, married and presented Manerd and "Al" with five top-notch grandchildren.

The Gaylers owned and operated many ranches during their career. All were part of the "romance" of ranching. (A hell of a lot of hard work!) However, the T4 Ranch near Nogales was home base for twenty-six years.

Manerd was a respected cattleman, well-liked by every-one, with a great sense of humor. He never retired until his body "plumb gave out." His last few days on this earth were filled with family and friends, and the way of life that none of us can seem to "shake loose." (He kept asking Alice to wrangle his horse!) She complied in her wonderful way, and wrangled that last horse just before their 50th anniversary.

We all miss you, Manerd. You enriched our lives, and made us damn proud to be your friend.

THE LAST OF THE SILVER SCREEN COWBOYS

Rex Allen and Koko

AN EXPERT IN HIS FIELD DOESN'T GIVE ANY
THOUGHT TO SECOND PLACE

Rex was the ultimate in western singing, a master of resonance. We miss his singing and can't understand how it's possible to buy C.D's featuring every artist, except Rex. There's got to be a way, Rex!

It's always fun and the highlight of a day to stop by Rex's place near Sonoita, Arizona, for a visit. Just the sound of his voice and his ever-present chuckle can brighten any day.

In one of our visits, Rex made mention that my uncle, Everett Bowman, was one of his heroes. Rex said that one of the more pleasant experiences of his many years of highway travel with his famous horse Koko was when Everett, then an Arizona State Highway patrolman, stopped him for speeding near Wickenberg, Arizona. They hadn't seen each other for several years. Rex instantly recognized Everett, but Everett wasn't sure who Rex was. Everett asked, "Are you a cowboy"? Rex replied, "Well, I was once." That broke the ice; they got reacquainted, sat down on the side of the road and had a helluva visit. Rex told me, "Ya know, when we both finally went on our separate ways, Everett had forgotten to write out my speeding ticket!"

One of my proudest possessions is an autographed picture of Rex that he gave to me many years ago when he was in his prime as an entertainer. Written on it is, "Lewis, they say you can count your real friends on one hand, call me a finger." What an honor it is to be called "Friend" by this fella and have him included in my list of heroes.

**SAVE THE WORD "FRIEND" FOR
THE ONES WHO WERE THERE WHEN
YOU NEEDED THEM**

Golf

HALL OF FAMERS COMPETE

After mastering just about everything there was for a cowboy to do, and whipping cancer surgery, Everett Bowman took up golf after retiring from professional rodeo competition in 1947. His natural athleticism and competitiveness prevailed; he became a reputable golfer after about a year of practice.

He and Babe Didrickson Zaharias, LPGA Hall of Fame Honoree in 1951, and also a winner over cancer surgery, pose at their charity benefit golf match at Wickenberg, Arizona, in 1952.

GOLF, AS DESCRIBED BY WINSTON CHURCHILL; "THE OBJECT OF THE GAME IS TO KNOCK A VERY SMALL BALL INTO A VERY SMALL HOLE WITH INSTRUMENTS ILL-DESIGNED TO ACHIEVE THE TASK."

NO WONDER MORE COWBOYS ARE PLAYIN' GOLF... GREEN GRASS AND WATER HOLES ARE SURE ADICTIN'

ALWAYS REMEMBER... LAUGHTER IS A UNIVERSAL LANGUAGE

WHEN YOU GET YOUR TARGET IN YOUR SIGHTS... BE SURE YOU HAVE MADE UP YOUR MIND WHETHER OR NOT TO PULL THE TRIGGER....

Everett Bowman and Babe Zaharias "ham it up" at their charity golf match at Wickenberg, Arizona, in 1952.

Babe, probably America's first sports heroine, and one of the world's greatest female athletes, broke four women's world records in track and field events in the 1932 Olympic Games. She excelled in baseball, basketball, skeet and rifle shooting, and was the title holder of three Women's Open Golf Tournaments.

With her dynamic personality, Babe was the firing pin of the budding Ladies Professional Golf Association in the 1940's and 50's, winning a dozen LPGA events in 1950 and 1951.

Everett's summation of their match golf play was, "I competed against many tough suckers in the rodeo arena, but never came across a more tenacious competitor than Babe."

**A GOLFER WITHOUT A SENSE OF HUMOR
IS OPERATIN' WITH A BIGGER HANDICAP THAN
A COWBOY WITHOUT A PAIR OF SPURS**

**WHEN YA HAND THE SCORE CARD TO A
COWBOY ON THE GOLF COURSE, YER *APT*
TO GET SOMETHIN' BACK THAT YOU'LL WANT
TO TELL YER GRAND-KIDS ABOUT**

SILENCE IS GOLDEN..
ESPECIALLY ON THE
GOLF COURSE

WILL ROGERS DEFINED A GENTLEMAN ON THE GOLF
COURSE AS; "ONE WHO LETS A LOST BALL STOP
ROLLING BEFORE HE PICKS IT UP"

BELIEVE IT OR NOT... THERE IS LIFE AFTER
GOLF AND ROPIN'....

WHEN YA SET OUT TO *BREAK PAR...*
BE SURE YA GET OFF THE *TEE....*

THE NAME OF THE GAME OF GOLF IS
"HOW MANY" NOT "HOW"

A GOLF GAME CAN BE PLAYED IN THREE OR
FOUR HOURS... BUT IT TAKES TWICE THAT LONG
TO TELL ABOUT IT....

YOU CAN READ A MAN'S CHARACTER A HELLUVA
LOT QUICKER ON A GOLF COURSE THAN YOU
CAN IN MOST PLACES

SOME GOLFERS HAVE ITCHY TRIGGER
FINGERS WHEN PUTTING....

CATTLE TRADERS REPORTING THE COW
MARKET HAVE PRODUCED MORE LIARS THAN GOLF

BETTIN' ON YER GOLF GAME WITH A FELLER THAT
WEARS SQUARE-TOED SHOES CAN BE HAZARDOUS

A GENTLEMAN ON THE GOLF COURSE LIMITS THE
NUMBER OF FOOT MASHIE SHOTS HE MAKES

A BAD DAY ON THE GOLF COURSE BEATS HELL
OUT OF GOOD DAY ON A NON-SATISFYING JOB...

TO WATCH MOST GOLFERS PUTTING MAKES YA
WANNA STOP THE WORLD AND GET OFF....

HOW COME A QUARTERBACK IS PLEASED WITH 60%
OF COMPLETED PASSES... A BATTER HITTING .300...
A BRONC RIDER SCORING 80... BUT A GOLFER
EXPECTS 100% ALL THE TIME?....

YOU BEGIN TO WONDER IF THE GREATEST
COWBOYS AND PUTTERS OF THE GOLF BALL ARE
BORN... NOT MADE....

WHEN YA GET TO FIGHTIN' YER GOLF GAME,
JUST THINK HOW LUCKY YOU ARE TO BE THERE...

THE MULLIGAN IS AN IRISH GIFT TO
A SCOTTISH GAME....

NINETEENTH HOLE = INSTANT REPLAY

YA GOTTA HIT IT BEFORE YA CHIP IT,
PITCH IT, SPLASH IT AND ROLL IT....

WHEN THE *WHEELS COME OFF* IN YER GOLF GAME,
KEEP SWINGIN' AND DON'T *KICK LOOSE*....

IT'S HARD TO PLAY YOUR HOME COURSE FROM
MEMORY WHEN YER BALL KEEPS GOIN'
PLACES YOU NEVER SAW BEFORE....

BELIEVE IT OR NOT... THERE ARE A LOT OF COWBOY
GOLFERS... SOME OF THEM PLAY LIKE IT, TOO....

WHEN YA GOT EXTRA MOVIN' PARTS IN YER GOLF
SWING, THERE'S NO DAMN TELLIN' WHERE YER
BALL WILL GO....

A BAD SHOT ON THE GOLF COURSE MAKES SOME
GOLFERS SO *DISCOMBOBULATED* THEY CAN'T
MAKE THEMSELVES REALIZE THAT LAST
SHOT IS GONE FOREVER

TOO MANY GOLFERS HAVE TO CONDUCT INTENSIVE
PERPENDICULAR, GEOLOGICAL AND
METEORLOGICAL SURVEYS BEFORE THEY CAN EVER
CONSIDER SWINGIN' AT THEIR BALL

THE FAIRWAY HAS BEEN DESCRIBED AS BEING
AT LEAST A FOOT AWAY FROM YOUR GOLF BALL

HOW DO YOU SUPPOSE A BASKETBALL PLAYER CAN
MAKE A SHOT AMIDST ALL THAT CONFUSION,
AND THE GOLFER HAS TO WAIT FOR THE WORLD TO
STOP SPINNING BEFORE HE CAN TAKE A STROKE?

SOME GOLFERS HAVE DESCRIBED AN AFTER DEATH
EXPERIENCE AFTER TAKING EIGHT STROKES TO GET
OUT OF A BUNKER

GOLF CAN GET SOME FELLAS SO *RATTLED* THEY
CAN'T FIND THEIR BUTT WITH BOTH HANDS

WHEN THE MODERN GOLFER BRAGS ABOUT HIS
OVERSIZED HEAD... LOOK AT HIS DRIVER..
NOT HIS HAT SIZE

THINK ABOUT IT... A CORD OF WOOD TO WARM
YOUR HOME COST $150.00 ... A CORD
OF GOLF TEES COSTS $24,000.00

THE FELLER WHO HAS NEVER PLAYED GOLF
HAS MISSED A LOT OF LIVIN'....

A MOMENT OF SILENCE FOR THE "GOLF WIDOWS"...
THEN WE'LL TEE OFF

HITTIN' A GOOD DRIVE IS LIKE CATCHIN' A CALF
WITH YER FIRST LOOP... IT DANG SURE HELPS YA
FORGET THE ONES YA MISSED

DO YOU SUPPOSE THERE'S A *TRANSDERMAL* GOLF
PATCH ON THE MARKET?

THE GAME OF GOLF HAS BEEN REFERRED
TO AS COW PASTURE POOL....

Bumfuzzled
Quips & Brands

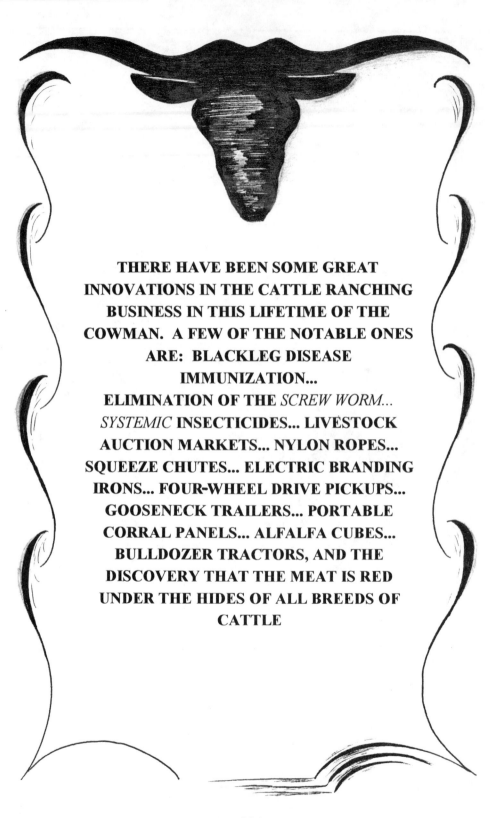

THERE HAVE BEEN SOME GREAT
INNOVATIONS IN THE CATTLE RANCHING
BUSINESS IN THIS LIFETIME OF THE
COWMAN. A FEW OF THE NOTABLE ONES
ARE: BLACKLEG DISEASE
IMMUNIZATION...
ELIMINATION OF THE *SCREW WORM...*
SYSTEMIC INSECTICIDES... LIVESTOCK
AUCTION MARKETS... NYLON ROPES...
SQUEEZE CHUTES... ELECTRIC BRANDING
IRONS... FOUR-WHEEL DRIVE PICKUPS...
GOOSENECK TRAILERS... PORTABLE
CORRAL PANELS... ALFALFA CUBES...
BULLDOZER TRACTORS, AND THE
DISCOVERY THAT THE MEAT IS RED
UNDER THE HIDES OF ALL BREEDS OF
CATTLE

THE VETERAN COWMAN WAS ASKED TO NAME
THE THREE BEST YEARS HE HAD SEEN IN
THE CATTLE BUSINESS. HE REPLIED,
"1941, 1958, AND THIS NEXT ONE."

YA CAN'T MAKE A SILK PURSE OUT
OF A SOW'S EAR

WHEN YA GET A *BIT IN YER TEETH,* BE SURE
YA KNOW WHERE YOU'RE HEADED

SOMETIMES IT PAYS TO
RATTLE A MAN'S CAGE

YA KNOW YOU'RE GETTIN' OLD WHEN YA
TURN THE LIGHT OUT FOR REST... RATHER
THAN ROMANCE

A ROUNDUP ISN'T TOO SUCCESSFUL WHEN THE
CATTLE GET
SCATTERED FROM HELL TO BREAKFAST

IF YA DON'T MEAN IT DON'T SAY IT....

WATCH OUT FOR A COWARD; HE'S MORE
DANGEROUS THAN A *SPOILED* HORSE

IF YA THINK YOU'VE NEVER BEEN WRONG,
YA HAVEN'T SPENT MUCH
BRAIN FODDER THINKIN'

**TIME AND TIDES DON'T FOOL AROUND...
THEY COME SURE AS HELL**

**MAKIN' A LIVIN' IN THE COW BUSINESS KEEPS
YA** *SUCKIN' THE HIND TIT*

**TOO BAD A FELLER CAN'T PICK
HIS RELATIVES**

**WHEN YA GET TO FEELIN' SAD ABOUT GETTIN'
OLDER WITH EACH DAY, JUST THINK ABOUT
THE ALTERNATIVE**

WHEN EVERYTHING'S *OUT OF KILTER,*
BACK UP AND MAKE ANOTHER *SCALD*

**IF YA SET OUT TO DRIVE A WEDGE, BE SURE YA
GET STARTED IN THE RIGHT SEAM**

**ANY PERSON WHO LOVES
HORSES, DOGS, AND LITTLE KIDS HAS
GOT TO BE OK**

IF IT DON'T HURT... IT DON'T WORK....

**WONDER WHY CHILI SAUCE IS ALWAYS
ATTRACTED TO EXPENSIVE NECK TIES?**

A *SQUIRRELY* **HORSE CAN MAKE YA
PLAY YER** *HOLE CARD*

LONGEVITY MEANS TOMORROW BECOMES TODAY

WHEN YA *BITE THE DUST,* **ALL YA CAN DO IS BRUSH THE DUST OFF, CRAWL BACK ON, AND GIVE 'ER** *ANOTHER WHIRL*

IT'S TOO BAD THEY HAVEN'T BEEN ABLE TO INSTALL COMMON SENSE INTO A COMPUTER PROGRAM

COWMEN MIND THEIR OWN *RAT KILLIN'* **AND GO TO THE POLLS**

SOMETIMES IT PAYS TO SIT WITH YER BACK TO THE WALL

MOST *DOGIES* **TURN OUT LOOKIN' LIKE THEY'VE BEEN HIT IN THE HEAD WITH A** *CHURN DASH*

SOME COWBOYS "DRIVE" CATTLE... OTHERS "PUSH" 'EM... TEXANS "CARRY" 'EM... THE BEST "POINT" 'EM

WHEN YA *SPILL* **A CATTLE DRIVE, YOU'VE DAMN SURE PULLED A** *BADDER ASS*

READ WHAT WILL ROGERS HAD TO SAY IF YA DON'T BELIEVE HISTORY REPEATS ITSELF

WHEN SIPPING THE FINEST OF VINTAGE
WINES, REMEMBER WHO PICKED UP THE TAB

DON'T UNDERESTIMATE THE WORTH OF A
RANCH WIFE

JUST GO ANOTHER MILE WHEN YA THINK YER
AT THE END OF YER ROPE

A SUCCESSFUL MAN'S CAREER IS LIKE THE
FLIGHT OF A BIRD... IT HAS PURPOSE AND
DETERMINATION

THERE ARE TOO MANY POLITICIANS AND TOO
FEW STATESMEN

THERE'S NO JOB TOUGHER THAN IDLENESS

MOST LIVESTOCK AUCTIONEERS ARE LIKE A
GRAVEYARD... THEY'LL TAKE ANYTHING

SAVE THE WORD "FRIEND" FOR THE ONES
WHO WERE THERE WHEN YA NEEDED THEM

PLANT YER OWN GARDEN INSTEAD OF
WAITING FOR SOMEONE TO BRING YA
FLOWERS

WHEN YA *STEAL A RIDE* ON A *SKITTISH HORSE*
YER NOT MAKIN' THE BEST *HAND*

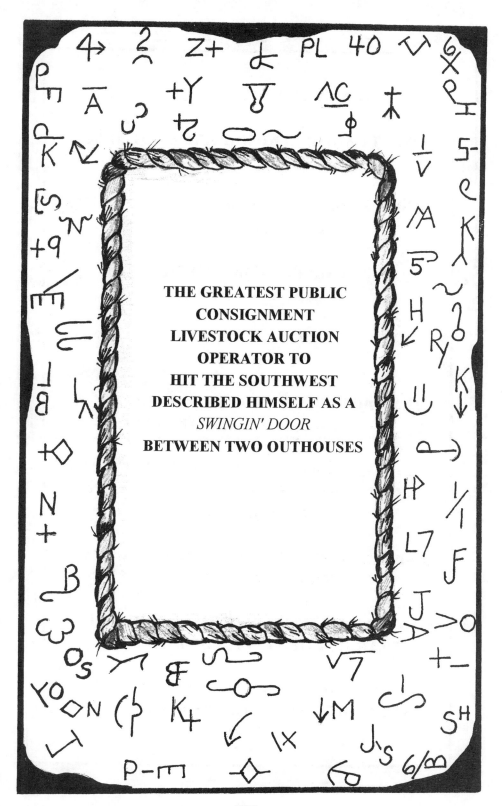

THE GREATEST PUBLIC
CONSIGNMENT
LIVESTOCK AUCTION
OPERATOR TO
HIT THE SOUTHWEST
DESCRIBED HIMSELF AS A
SWINGIN' DOOR
BETWEEN TWO OUTHOUSES

IT DOESN'T PAY TO THROW *KNIPTION FITS*

LOYALTY AND FRIENDSHIP ARE A LOT ALIKE...
YA CAN'T BUY EITHER ONE....

SHORT BRIDLE REINS AND STIFF *LATTIGOS* CAN
JUST PLAIN *GRAB YA*

EVEN A BLIND SQUIRREL FINDS A NUT
ONCE IN AWHILE

DON'T *CUT MUCH SLACK* TO THE ONE THAT
FUDGES

IF YA DON'T HAVE SWEATY PALMS ONCE IN
AWHILE, SOMETHIN'S MISSIN'

RIDIN' A *COLD JAWED* HORSE IS WORSE THAN
RIDIN' A *COLD JAWED* MULE... YA EXPECT IT
FROM THE MULE

IT SURE IS HARD TO DIAPER A BABY WHEN YER
WEARIN' BOXIN' GLOVES

DAD TOLD ME THERE WOULD BE SOME TOUGH
DAYS, BUT HE NEVER SAID HOW MANY

JUST MAKIN' A LOT OF TRACKS DOESN'T
NECESSARILY MEAN YOU'RE GETTIN' A LOT
DONE

**WHEN YOU'RE ON THE ROAD TO SUCCESS...
BE SURE THERE'S NOT A BRIDGE OUT....**

**THERE WAS NEVER A PERSON BORN ROTTEN...
THE BAD ONES HAD TO LEARN THAT
SOMEWHERE**

**YA NEVER SOLVE A PROBLEM BY JUST
STICKIN' YER HEAD IN THE SAND**

**HOUSE GUESTS ARE LIKE FISH... THEY START
TO SMELL AFTER THREE DAYS**

**WHEN YA STAND FIRMLY ON PRINCIPLE,
YOU CAN LET SOME COMMON SENSE
GET AWAY**

**IT'S BEST TO BUILD YER ROADS TODAY...
CAUSE TOMORROW'S GROUND AIN'T TOO
CERTAIN**

**BEFORE YA TAKE A JOB THAT PAYS YOU WHAT
YER WORTH, BE SURE YA CAN LIVE ON
THAT WAGE**

**NOTHIN' CAN STOP YA WHEN YA PUT LOTS OF
BACK JUICE TOGETHER WITH *BRAIN FODDER***

**NOTHIN' COMPARES TO THE INNOCENCE OF
THE YOUNG**

DON'T STUMP YER TOE OVER A DOLLAR TO
PICK UP A NICKEL

IF YA TAKE CARE OF THE LITTLE THINGS, YA
PROBABLY WON'T HAVE MANY BIG ONES TO
WORRY ABOUT

IF IT AIN'T WORTH DOIN' RIGHT...
IT AIN'T WORTH DOIN'....

BOSSES WHO RUN IN CIRCLES SHALL BE
KNOWN AS WHEELS

EVERYBODY'S GOTTA HAVE SOMEBODY

INDECISION IS LIKE HAVIN' A ROCK IN
YER BOOT

WHEN YER RUNNIN' THE SHOW, KEEP YER
EAR TO THE GROUND

THERE IS NO SUBSTITUTE FOR COMMITMENT

TO SOME COWBOYS, INTERNAL COMBUSTION
MEANS TOO MANY HOURS
SPENT AT THE BAR

TRYIN' TO REASON WITH A BUREAUCRAT IS
LIKE ROLLIN' YER OWN CIGARETTES IN A
HIGH WIND

MIXIN' YER CATTLE WITH FUTURES MARKET CONTRACTS CAN BE LIKE REARRANGIN' THE SPARKPLUG WIRES ON YER TRUCK ENGINE

A MAN IS AWARE OF HIS OWN SHORTCOMINGS... DEALING WITH THEM IS HIS PROBLEM

THE AMERICAN DREAM IS NOT OWNING YER OWN HOME, IT'S GETTING YER KIDS OUT OF IT

THE TOMATO CANS THAT SOME COWBOYS COME UP WITH FER BELT BUCKLES ARE SOMETHIN' TO TELL YER GRANDKIDS ABOUT

THE LIVESTOCK AUCTION ORDER BUYER WHO DOESN'T OWN A PENCIL SURE MAKES THE AVERAGE COWMAN FEEL INFERIOR

COUNT YER BLESSINGS EVERYDAY AND BE GRATEFUL THAT YOU'RE ABLE TO

THERE'S NOT A LOT OF DIFFERENCE BETWEEN THE HEIGHT OF AN EAGLE'S NEST AND A BUZZARD'S ROOST

SOMETHIN' IS *HAY WIRE* IN THE CATTLE AND BEEF INDUSTRIES WHEN YA CAN'T FIND A *HEIFER* STEAK IN CONSUMER BEEF OUTLETS

PUTTIN' A LITTLE *BRAHMAN* BLOOD IN YER
BEEF BREEDING PROGRAM IS LIKE PUTTIN' A
LITTLE SALT ON YER FOOD... IT ONLY
TAKES A TOUCH TO MAKE A *WHALE* OF A
DIFFERENCE

A FULL *MOUNT* OF *POTENT* HORSES CAN MAKE
A COWBOY WONDER WHAT OTHER
OCCUPATIONS ARE LIKE

ITS A SHAME THAT A BED OF ROSES IS ALWAYS
SO FULL OF THORNS

THE MAN WHO STRADDLES THE FENCE
GETS SPLINTERS IN HIS ASS

YA BETTER LET THE *SMOKE SETTLE* BEFORE YA
MAKE YER MOVE

IF YA THINK YOU'RE A TOP NOTCH TRADER,
JUST TRY SELLIN' WATER TO A DRUNK

DON'T TRADE WITH A FELLA THAT
RESERVES THE RIGHT TO CHANGE HIS MIND

WHEN YA HAVE A *RAZOO* WITH YER CATTLE...
YER IN A *STORM*

LOGIC AND REASON PRODUCE MORE RESULTS
THAN RULES AND DIRECTIVES

CATTLE RANCHERS AND FARMERS ARE
THE ONLY ONES IN THE BUSINESS WORLD
WHO BUY RETAIL, SELL WHOLESALE,
AND PAY THE FREIGHT BOTH WAYS

IN SOME PLACES THE NUMBER OF CATTLE
THAT CAN BE LOADED ON A TRUCK DEPENDS
ON HOW FAST THEY BRING EM' UP THE CHUTE

SOMETIMES IT PAYS FOR THE WEATHERMAN
TO STICK HIS HEAD OUT THE WINDOW BEFORE
MAKIN' A FORECAST

WHEN YA STAMP A MAN'S NAME ON YER
OUTHOUSE WALL, IT'S NOT ADVISABLE TO
BURN IT IN WITH A HOT IRON

WHEN YER AT THE *BOTTOM OF THE BARREL,*
THERE'S NO WAY TO GO BUT UP

BE CAREFUL YER FIRST WIN DOESN'T MAKE A
GAMBLER OUT OF YA

WHEN YA TAKE OFF *HALF-COCKED...* YOU'RE
SURE *APT* TO PULL A *BADDER ASS*

YA GOTTA GET YER FEET WET BEFORE YA CAN
GO SWIMMIN'

THE HOTTER THE TIP, THE MORE YA CAN GET
BURNED

WORKAHOLICS SHOULD BE CAREFUL THEY
DON'T GET TO LOOKIN' LIKE THEY'VE BEEN
DRUG THROUGH A KNOT HOLE

IT'S UNUSUAL WHEN A COWBOY GETS *BLIND SIDED* MORE THAN ONCE

MISSIN' THE ESTIMATED WEIGHT OF YER SALE CATTLE BY TWENTY POUNDS WHEN YOU'VE SOLD ON A *SLIDE* CONTRACT WILL BREAK YA FROM *SUCKIN' EGGS*

A MEAN BULL OR A CROOKED POLITICIAN CAN *PUT YA TO STOOPIN'*

YA BETTER NOT TAKE MUCH *OFF THE WALL* WHEN YOU'RE IN THE COW BUSINESS

TRYIN' TO MAKE A *FIRST STRINGER* OUT OF AN *IRON HEADED* HORSE IS LIKE SPITTIN' INTO THE WIND

EVERY WAGON NEEDS A GOOD *WHEEL HORSE* IN THE *HITCH*

IF YA KEEP SHOOTIN' YERSELF IN THE FOOT... YOU'LL FINALLY BLOW YER HEAD OFF

WHEN YA LEAD WITH YER CHIN YA CAN *PULL BACK A STUB*

CATTLE RANCHERS AND FARMERS WORK FROM DAYLIGHT TO DARK WITH MOTHER NATURE *CRACKIN' THE WHIP*

WHIP AND SPUR WHEN YA KNOW THERE'S A
BOG HOLE AHEAD

ONE OF THE KEYS TO SUCCESS IS TO PLAN YER
WORK THEN WORK YER PLAN

MOST LIVESTOCK LOAN BANKERS ARE
TIGHTER'N THE BARK ON A TREE

AN AMBIDEXTROUS COWBOY IS AS HANDY AS
A POCKET ON A SHIRT

WHEN THE CHIPS ARE DOWN YA FIND OUT
WHO YER TRUE FRIENDS ARE

MANY BEEF CATTLE PRODUCERS FEEL JUST
LIKE A PUPPET ON A STRING EVER SINCE
CATTLE FUTURES PAPER CONTRACTS WERE
INVENTED

EVERYBODY CAN'T BE A CHAMPION,
SOMEONE HAS TO CHEER FROM
THE SIDELINES

A FELLER THAT GETS TO FEELIN' SORRY FOR
HIMSELF NEVER EXCELS

ITS NOT TOO DESIRABLE TO DO BUSINESS
WITH A FELLER WHEN YA CONTINUALLY HAVE
TO *WATCH YER BACK*

THE BIGGEST EGOTISTS ARE NOT ALWAYS THE
BIGGEST WINNERS

ON A COLD RAINY DAY ON HORSEBACK...
YA CAN BET THERE'S A COWBOY WHO WISHES
HE HADN'T USED HIS *SLICKER* TO *SACK OUT* THE
COLTS

THE COWMAN WILL BE THERE *'TIL THE FAT
LADY SINGS*

WHEN A COWMAN WEANS 600 POUND CALVES...
HE'S *HITTIN' THE NAIL ON THE HEAD*

RIDIN' A *BARN SOURED* HORSE CAN MAKE A
COWBOY GOOFIER THAN A *PEACH ORCHARD
BOAR*

A FELLER'S FORMAL EDUCATION DOESN'T
AMOUNT TO MUCH WHEN HIS CURRICULUM
HASN'T TAKEN HIM PAST THE SAND BOX

COWPUNCHIN' IS LIKE CANCER... A DISEASE
THAT IS RARELY CURED

COWBOYS PLAIN DON'T LIKE GREASE, THE
OTHER STUFF WASHES OFF A LOT EASIER

TOO MUCH DRY WEATHER CAN MAKE A
COWMAN'S FINGERNAILS SWEAT

IF A COWMAN DOESN'T KNOW WHAT
HE'S GONNA DO IN THE MORNIN'...
HE BETTER HOPE HE DOESN'T MEET HIMSELF
COMIN' BACK

WHEN YER SITTIN' ON A HOT STOVE WITH YER
FEET IN COLD WATER... ON AN AVERAGE,
YOU'RE WARM

IT'S AMAZIN' HOW MANY OLD PEOPLE SHOW
UP FOR THEIR FIFTIETH CLASS REUNION

FINALLY FIGURED OUT WHY MY TWO SONS
DIDN'T FOLLOW MY FOOTSTEPS IN THE
COW BUSINESS; THEY WERE NEARLY
GROWN BEFORE THEY KNEW THE COLOR
OF A FAT COW

IT'S AMAZING HOW MUCH HARDER THE
GROUND IS NOW COMPARED TO WHAT IT WAS
SIXTY-SIX YEARS AGO

THE NAME OF THE GAME WHEN YA GET
YER CATTTLE SALE RECEIPTS ON A DOWN
MARKET IS
"READ 'EM AND WEEP"

KEEP THE LIGHT SWITCH HANDY...
YA NEVER KNOW WHEN YA MIGHT WANT TO
SHUT THINGS DOWN

SIGN ON AN
ANIMAL HEALTH
CLINIC

VETERINARIAN AND TAXIDERMIST

EITHER WAY YA GET
YER DOG BACK

MOTHER NATURE CALLS MOST OF THE
SHOTS IN THE COW BUSINESS

COUNTIN' YER BLESSINGS CAN DO A HELLUVA
LOT MORE FOR YA THAN CRYIN'
IN YER BEER

YOU HAVEN'T GOT MUCH IF THERE'S NO
HUMOR IN IT

IF YA DON'T KEEP A CLEAR CONSCIENCE,
YA COULD WIND UP SILLIER THAN A
STOMPED ANT

MOST OLDER FELLERS ARE EITHER TRYIN' TO
REMEMBER SOMEONE'S NAME OR HUNTIN' A
PLACE TO TAKE A LEAK

SOMETHIN'S *HAY WIRE* WHEN YOU HAVE TO
SLEEP WITH ONE EYE OPEN

WHEN YER IN A *STORM,* SOMETIMES IT PAYS
TO JUST *KICK* LOOSE

NO USE TRYIN' TO EXPLAIN NUCLEAR ENERGY
TO A COWBOY; DAMN FEW OF THEM HAVE
FIGGERED OUT THE LIGHT BULB

IF YA WANNA DANCE, YA GOT TO
PAY THE FIDDLER

THE TURTLE AND HARE PHILOSOPHY DOESN'T APPLY ON A COW RANCH... THE RANCH HARE NEVER GETS THAT MUCH REST

WHEN YA SET YER TRAPS, BE SURE THE MECHANICS ARE IN PLACE FOR WORKIN' THE TRAPLINE

MOST ARROGANCE HAS MORE BARK THAN BITE

WHEN YA GO FISHING, TAKE ALONG A BUCKET OF ROCKS TO BE SURE YOU'LL HAVE SOMETHIN' TO DO

FOR EVERY MAN-MADE PROBLEM THERE'S A MAN-MADE SOLUTION, WHICH APPLIES TO THE ABSENCE OF YOUR C.D.s, REX

THE DISCIPLINE OF YER WORK IS LIKE A HAND OF CARDS... YA CAN PLAY IT ANYWAY YA WANT TO

IT'S NO BIG DEAL TO STAND BY YER WORD... THAT SHOULD BE NATURAL FOR EVERYBODY

WHEN YA HAVE COMPANY IN THE EVENING, YA MIGHT WANT TO THINK ABOUT GOIN' TO BED... CAUSE YER COMPANY MIGHT WANNA GO HOME

ALL *HELL BREAKS LOOSE* **WHEN YER HERD**
STAMPEDES

**IT PAYS TO TEAR INTO THOSE REPULSIVE JOBS
LIKE YOU ARE FIGHTIN' SNAKES**

WHEN YA GET INVOLVED IN SOMEONE ELSE'S
RAT KILLIN', **YER OWN IS** *APT* **TO GO BEGGIN'**

**LIVE YER LIFE AS AN EXCLAMATION...
NOT AN EXPLANATION**

**BE CAREFUL YA DON'T RUST UP BEFORE YA
WEAR OUT**

**WHAT A FELLER BROUGHT WITH HIM IS NOT
AS IMPORTANT AS WHAT HE DOES WITH IT**

**THE GREATEST WEALTH A COWBOY
ACQUIRES IS THE
SATISFACTION OF ACCOMPLISHMENT**

**THE ONLY WAY OUT OF TROUBLE IS TO WORK
LIKE HELL UNTIL YOU'VE SLUGGED YER WAY
THROUGH IT**

**IT SURE IS TOUGH FOR A COWMAN TO
CONTINUALLY EXECUTE WHEN
MOTHER NATURE IS THE
QUARTERBACK**

A COWBOY CAN SPOT A PHONY
QUICKER THAN A DUCK ON A JUNE BUG

TRADERS ON WALL STREET ARE BUSIER THAN
A DOG IN A WAREHOUSE FULL OF FIRE PLUGS

IT'S PROBABLY TIME TO THINK ABOUT
ACQUIRING YOURSELF A KEEPER WHEN YA
REPEATEDLY OPEN THE ICEBOX DOOR, THEN
STAND THERE STARING IN, WONDERING WHAT
IN THE HELL YOU'RE DOIN' THERE

WHEN YOU'VE MADE YER FIRST CLASSIC
BRONC RIDE, YER PROBABLY AS SURPRIZED AS
A DOG WITH HIS FIRST PORCUPINE

THE CATTLE BUSINESS WILL BE THERE
'TIL THE LAST DOG IS HUNG

WHEN YOUR SADDLE HORSE GETS TO
LOOKING LIKE A *GUTTED SNOW BIRD,* YOU
KNOW YA HAVEN'T DONE A GOOD JOB

HOLDIN' A *DAY HERD* ON
A LONG HOT DAY CAN DO MORE
FOR YA THAN JUST TEST YER
STAYIN' POWER

THE WORST KIND OF BANKRUPTCY IS A
FELLER WHO HAS RUN OUT OF *ZIP*

BEFORE YOU'RE FITTED WITH GOLDEN
HANDCUFFS OR GOLDEN PARACHUTES YA
BETTER TAKE A LOOK AT YER *HOLE CARD*

MAKES NO DIFFERENCE WHICH WAY
THE WIND BLOWS, SOMEONE WILL BENEFIT
FROM IT

THE BIG PERCENTAGE OF MOST LIVESTOCK
BREEDING GOES RIGHT DOWN THE
OFF-SPRING'S THROAT

SURE WISH I HAD COME ALONG A LITTLE
SOONER... BEFORE THE ELECTRONIC
TELEPHONE ANSWERING SERVICE HAD BEEN
INVENTED

SOLVIN' THE PROBLEMS OF A CATTLE
OPERATION IS LIKE A
ROPIN' CONTEST... THROW WHEN YA GET
THERE

FOR OLDER COWBOYS, THE EASY RIDE OF
SOME HORSES CAN MAKE THEIR *ASS LAUGH*...
BUT THE ROUGH RIDE OF SOME OF THE OTHER
HORSES MAKE 'EM REALIZE THEY'VE
DEVELOPED THE *ROUND ASS*

PRIMETIME IN THE COW BUSINESS IS GREEN
GRASS AND GOOD MARKETS

**YA HAVE TO BE A BIG
FELLER TO PUSH THE
WRINKLES OUTA YER SHIRT**

IT'S A *SORRY* **MAN WHO SADDLES A**
GALDED **HORSE**

**TAX COLLECTORS ARE 'BOUT AS WELCOME AS
A SKUNK IN THE CHICKEN HOUSE**

NEVER SADDLE A HORSE WITH A *HITCH*
IN HIS GET-ALONG

**IT'LL BE A COLD DAY IN HELL WHEN YA
FIGGER OUT ALL OF MOTHER NATURE'S**
WRINKLES

WHEN YA *PUT YER MONEY WHERE YER MOUTH IS* ,
YA USUALLY HAVE A TRADE

**DON'T CARRY YER EMOTIONS AROUND ON
YER SHIRT SLEEVES**

**IN A TOUGH SPOT, YOU CAN FIND A PIECE OF
YERSELF YA DIDN'T KNOW WAS MISSIN'**

SOMETIMES IT PAYS TO *LET THE BARS DOWN*

**TIME IS ONE OF THE MOST VALUABLE THINGS
A FELLER'S GOT**

**POLITICIANS USUALLY HAVE TO BE TOUCHED
WITH A SLEDGEHAMMER BEFORE THEY GET
THE MESSAGE**

IT'S TIME TO LOOK FOR A *BUGGER* WHEN A FELLER INSISTS ON GIVING YOU SOMETHING FREE

YA DON'T ALWAYS HAVE TO SAY SOMETHING ON EVERY SUBJECT AND ON EVERY OCCASION

IT PAYS TO BE THOUGHTFUL BUT NOT MOODY; HELPFUL BUT NOT BOSSY

IF A COWMAN COULD RUN HIS RANCH TO THE BEST ADVANTAGE OF THE IRS RULES INSTEAD OF THE DICTATES OF MOTHER NATURE, HE MIGHT STAND A SLIM CHANCE OF BEING FINANCIALLY COMPETITIVE WITH SOME OF THE OTHER BUSINESSES

WHAT A LOT OF SUCCESSFUL MEN LACKED BETWEEN THEIR EARS, THEY MADE UP FOR WITH THEIR BACK

THERE'S NO SIN IN NOT SUCCEEDING... THE SIN IS NOT TRYING

DON'T KEEP PROMOTIN' NEW DEALS... MAKE YOUR GOOD ONES PRODUCE

THE DIFFERENCE BETWEEN A PROMOTER AND A PRODUCER; THE PROMOTER SETS 'EM UP, THE PRODUCER KNOCKS 'EM DOWN

TOO MANY FAMOUS PEOPLE DEVELOP
ROOT ROT

THE SUCCESS OF MOST CATTLE RANCHERS CAN BE TRACED TO THEIR WIVES... WHO HAD JOBS IN TOWN

THERE IS NO PERFECTIONIST LIKE A VIRGO

THE FIRST LESSON THAT LIVESTOCK BRAND INSPECTORS AND LIVESTOCK TRUCK DRIVERS NEED TO MASTER IS HOW TO READ A CLOCK

IT'S HARD TO FIGURE WHY YA HAVE TO PAY UNCLE SAM BEFORE YA BUY BABY SHOES AND SCHOOL BOOKS

FEDERAL "CATTLE ON FEED REPORTS" ARE AS WORTHLESS AS A WOODPECKER WITH A HEADACHE

EXCESSIVELY TALKATIVE COWBOYS, USUALLY DUBBED "GABBY" OR "BREEZY," CAN MAKE SO MUCH NOISE IT WOULD GIVE A BOILERMAKER THE JITTERS

DAILY STUDY OF THE LIVESTOCK FUTURES MARKET CAN MAKE THE AVERAGE COWMAN MORE *SKIDDISH* THAN A LONG TAILED CAT IN A ROOM FULL OF ROCKING CHAIRS

WHEN YA THINK YA AIN'T GOT WHAT IT
TAKES... *HANG TOUGH*

WHEN THE WATER TANK RUNS OVER, YA
ALWAYS WONDER WHEN THE BOSS
WILL HOLLER TO TURN THE PUMP OFF

YER PERFORMANCE IS ALWAYS BEIN'
EVALUATED BY SOMEONE

WHEN YA LOSE YER ABILITY TO TAKE A RISK
YOU'VE 'BOUT LOST THE WHOLE
SHOOTIN' MATCH

THERE'S PLENTY OF PRIDE IN PAYIN' YER
OWN WAY

WHEN YA GOT A SQUARE PLUG FER A ROUND
HOLE... YA GOT MORE THAN A LITTLE
PROBLEM

A COWBOY SHOULDN'T GO ANYWHERE
WITHOUT A ROPE, A POCKET KNIFE, SOME
BALIN' WIRE AND A BUCKET OF
ALFALFA CUBES

WHEN YER UP TO YER ASS IN COWSHIT,
IT'S A LITTLE LATE TO REMIND
YOURSELF THAT IT'S TIME TO CLEAN
THE CORRAL

EVEN IF YOU DON'T HAVE ANYTHING TO DO...
GET AFTER IT....

WHEN YA GOT A *GREEN* COWBOY IN YER CREW
THAT'S NOT *DRY BEHIND THE EARS,* YER SURE
GONNA HAVE TO DO SOME SCHOOL TEACHIN'

THE BATTLE CRY OF A MAN IN AGRICULTURE...
NEXT YEAR!!!

DON'T EVER HIRE A MAN THAT WEARS
GLOVES, ROLLS HIS OWN CIGARETTES AND
WEARS A STRAW HAT

DON'T FLINCH WHEN YA SHOOT FROM THE HIP

WHEN YA SHAKE HANDS WITH A FELLER, BE
SURE YA DON'T LEAVE HIM WITH THE FEELING
THAT HE JUST GOT HOLD OF A DEAD FISH

LEAD.. FOLLOW... OR GET OUT OF THE WAY

ONE YOUNG BOY IS GOOD HELP..
TWO BOYS ARE PRETTY GOOD HELP...
THREE BOYS AREN'T MUCH HELP AT ALL

YOUTH DEFICIENCY IS THE WORST DRAW
BACK TO OLD AGE

GIVE CREDIT WHERE CREDIT IS DUE

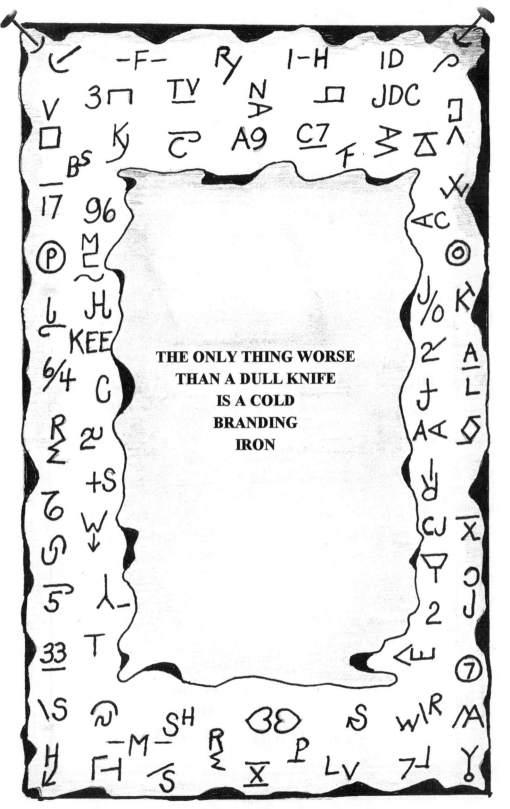

THE ONLY THING WORSE
THAN A DULL KNIFE
IS A COLD
BRANDING
IRON

'BOUT EVERY FEW YEARS THERE'S A HELLUVA
WRECK IN THE CATTLE MARKET THAT SURE
SETS THE HAIR ON A COWMAN,
BUT HE ALWAYS SEEMS TO
HEAL UP AND HAIR OVER

THE COWMAN WILL BE THERE *'TIL*
THE FAT LADY SINGS

A COWMAN IS NEVER ABLE TO PAY A GOOD
COWBOY WHAT HE'S WORTH... A *SORRY* ONE
IS ALWAYS OVERPAID

THE POPULARITY OF A BREED OF CATTLE IS AS
UNSTABLE AS A WOMAN'S HEM LINE

WHEN YA TAKE A *DIVE ASS* JUST *GATHER*
YOURSELF AND CRAWL BACK ON

YA KNOW YOU'RE GETTIN' OLD WHEN YA
SEEM TO KNOW MOST OF THE ANSWERS, BUT
CAN'T THINK OF ANY NEW QUESTIONS

WHEN YA GET ON A SOAP BOX, DON'T GET
HYPNOTIZED BY THE SOUND OF YER
OWN VOICE

THERE'S A WEALTH OF INFORMATION IN A
COWMAN'S *LITTLE BLACK BOOK,* BUT HE'S THE
ONLY ONE THAT CAN DECIPHER IT.

A GOOD RAINY SEASON ISN'T THE SOLE
FACTOR THAT CREATES ECONOMIC STABILITY
FOR THE CATTLEMAN

TAKE CARE OF THE NICKELS AND THE
DOLLARS WILL TAKE CARE
OF THEMSELVES

TO SUCCEED YA GOTTA GET PREPARATION
AND OPPORTUNITY TOGETHER

STICKIN' YER FOOT IN YER MOUTH CAN MAKE
YA THINK ABOUT *RUNNIN' BACKWARDS*

THE BEST ROPIN'S EVER WON ALWAYS SEEM
TO BE THE FARTHEST FROM HOME

NINE MONTHS OF DROUTH WILL *TAKE THE
SLACK OUT* OF YER ROPE

IT SURE WOULD BE HELPFUL IF THEY MADE A
COMPUTER SYSTEM THAT REQUIRED
OPERATORS TO USE THEIR HEAD
WHILE THEY'RE PUNCHIN' BUTTONS

SOME HORSE TRADERS ARE SO SLICK THEY
COULD SELL ICE TO AN ESKIMO

YA DON'T CALL A MAN A FRIEND WHO SELLS
YA A COUNTERFEIT HORSE

WHEN YER RIDIN' HIGH WIDE AND HANDSOME,
DON'T FORGET THE PEOPLE WHO BROUGHT
YA TO THE DANCE

WHEN YA *PLAY YER CARDS CLOSE TO YER CHEST,*
BE SURE THE *SPITTOON STAYS IN THE MIDDLE*
OF THE TABLE

SOME SITUATIONS REQUIRE A *STICK OF
POWDER* AND A SHORT FUSE

COWBOYS DON'T MAKE MISTAKES, THEY
PULL *BADDER ASSES*

A SUDDEN DRASTIC DROP IN THE CATTLE
MARKET CAN SURE *JERK THE PROPS OUT*
FROM UNDER A COWMAN

YELLOW JOURNALISM MUST HAVE REACHED THE
BOTTOM OF THE BARREL, IT IS WORKING
ON THE *MECHANICS* OF THE
RANCHING BUSINESS NOW

RANCHERS HAVE BEEN CALLED "RUGGED
INDIVIDUALISTS"... THEY BETTER
QUEDOW THEY DON'T BECOME
"RAGGED INDISCRIMINATES"

FOR MANY COWBOYS, THE OLDER THEY GET
THE MORE FACE THEY HAVE TO WASH

IF YER BURNIN' THE CANDLE AT BOTH ENDS,
YA MIGHT BE LUCKY IF IT HAS A
FAULTY WICK

WHEN YA SEE A LIGHT AT THE END OF THE
TUNNEL, MAKE SURE IT'S NOT A TRAIN COMIN'

IF IT DOESN'T CONTAIN LEATHER OR HORSE
HAIR, NO USE TRYIN' TO EXPLAIN IT TO
A COWBOY

PLENTY OF GREEN GRASS CAN CREATE A
FALSE SENSE OF SECURITY FOR A CATTLEMAN

YA CAN'T REACH THE TOP OF THE LADDER
WITHOUT FEELIN' SOME PRIDE

TUNNEL VISION IS OK IF YA HAVE A ONE
TRACK MIND

WHEN YA GOT A HALF A CUP... BE SURE IT'S
HALF FULL... NOT HALF EMPTY

GIVE A COWMAN LOTS OF GREEN GRASS AND
A CHECK BOOK, AND HE CAN BECOME THE
BIGGEST FOOL IN THE WORLD

THERE'S A BIG DIFFERENCE BETWEEN
BREAKIN' A GATE DOWN AND RIDIN' THROUGH
AN OPEN ONE

BEFORE YA GET OUT ON A LIMB, BE SURE
THERE'S NOBODY AROUND WITH A SAW

IF YA DON'T BELIEVE TIME CHANGES
EVERYTHING, JUST STICK AROUND AWHILE

RULES ARE MADE WHEN BRAINS RUN OUT....

THE COWMAN ON NOAH'S ARK
MADE ONE REMARK WHEN
THEY LANDED;
"GEE WHIZ, ANOTHER SHOWER LIKE THIS IN
A DAY OR TWO, AND WE COULD SURE HAVE A
GOOD YEAR"

ALWAYS PLAY YER CARDS ON TOP OF THE
TABLE

A GOOD HORSE IS LIKE A GOOD WOMAN...
HARD TO COME BY....

NOT ALL LIVESTOCK LOAN BANKERS ARE
LIKE A GOOD COWBOY... IN THE RIGHT PLACE
AT THE RIGHT TIME

A NOVICE TRADING IN CATTLE FUTURE
CONTRACTS PROBABLY WON'T LAST AS LONG
AS A PAPER SHIRT IN A BEAR FIGHT

STEP EASY ON THIN ICE

THE COW BUSINESS IS MOSTLY ONE DAMN WRECK AFTER ANOTHER

THE BUSINESS OF RAISIN' CATTLE IS SURELY NOT UNEVENTFUL

WHEN YER WRONG... WONDER WHO'S THE
FIRST TO KNOW IT

FOOTBALL IS LIKE RODEO... IT DOESN'T TAKE
LONG TO SEPARATE THE MEN FROM THE BOYS

IT SURE WOULD BE SOMETHIN' IF A COWMAN
COULD OWN HIS CALVES FROM THE TIME
THEY LEFT THE RANCH UNTIL THEY GOT ON
SOMEBODY'S DINNER PLATE

COWBOYS RAISED IN THE SOUTHWEST FIND
NORTHERN SEASONS TO RUN NINE MONTHS OF
WINTER AND THREE MONTHS LATE IN
THE FALL

IT USUALLY DOESN'T PAY TO *CUT MUCH SLACK*
TO A HORSE THAT KEEPS *FALLIN' APART*

SOMETHIN' SEEMS OUT OF GEAR WHEN
NON-FERROUS, NON-EDIBLE METALS, SELL
FOR A HIGHER PRICE PER POUND THAN MANY
LIFE-SUSTAINING FOODS

TRYIN' TO COVER UP A *BADDER ASS* WILL ONLY
GET YA IN MANURE OVER YER *HOCKS*

YA CAN'T HAVE YER CAKE AND EAT IT TOO,
BUT YOU CAN GIVE YER WORD AND STILL
KEEP IT

WHEN OLDER FELLERS HAVE TO GIVE UP HALF
OF THEIR SEX LIFE, IT'S IMPORTANT THEY
SELECT THE RIGHT HALF; THE HALF OF
THINKIN' ABOUT IT OR THE HALF OF TALKIN'
ABOUT IT

WHILE SHUFFLIN' PAPERS BE SURE YA DON'T
LOSE TRACK OF THE BALL

IF YER GONNA BE A GENERAL, COME OFF YER
PERCH ONCE IN AWHILE AND ACT LIKE A
PRIVATE

SOME FELLER'S HAVE TO KEEP AN EXTRA
ROOM TO STORE THEIR EGO

IT'S AMAZIN' HOW MUCH FURTHER YA CAN
SEE WHEN YA HOLD YER HEAD UP

IF YER GONNA TAKE THE LEAD, DON'T DO IT
JUST TO SATISFY YER EGO

CINCH UP ANOTHER NOTCH WHEN THINGS
GET TOUGH

THERE'S NOTHIN' WRONG WITH CONFIDENCE...
JUST DON'T OVERUSE IT....

SWEAT MARKS WILL PRODUCE MORE
THAN A SLICK HIDE

COWBOYS KEEP SEARCHIN' FOR THAT ROMANCE THAT'S SUPPOSED TO BE PART OF *PUNCHIN' COWS*

COW PUNCHERS AND SHEEP HERDERS ARE ABOUT AS COMPATIBLE AS TWO STRANGE BULLDOGS

A MAN HAS A LOT OF *BOTTOM* **WHEN HE HANDLES HIS TROUBLES WITHOUT COMPLAININ'**

YA CAN'T BE HIGHLY SUCCESSFUL IF YER ALWAYS STEALIN' SOMEBODY ELSE'S *THUNDER*

WHEN YA THINK YOU'RE GITTIN' TO THE *END OF YER ROPE, SPUR* **UP A LITTLE AND GET A LITTLE MORE SLACK**

WHEN ONE OF YER TEAM KEEPS JUMPIN' THE *TRACES,* **MIGHT BE A GOOD IDEA TO SHORTIN' HIS** *TRACE*

DON'T REMEMBER FOR SURE WHAT CAUSED THE FALL OF THE ROMAN EMPIRE, BUT AMERICA BETTER KEEP AN EYE ON BUREAUCRACY AND COMPUTERS

IT'S HARD TO GET ANYTHING DONE WHEN EVERYTHING IS *OUT OF KILTER*

A SENSE OF HUMOR CAN PRODUCE MORE
RICHES THAN YOU CAN *TALLY*

WHEN YA GET TO FEELIN' SORRY FOR
YERSELF, JUST STOP AND LOOK AROUND

IF THE YOUNG HAD ANY IDEA WHAT WAS
AHEAD, THEY'D PUT SOME OF THAT YOUTH IN
A BOTTLE AND SAVE IT FOR LATER

IT PAYS TO LET YER RIGHT HAND KNOW WHAT
YER LEFT HAND IS DOIN'

DRIVIN' DRAGS ON A DUSTY TRAIL CAN TEACH
YA MORE THAN JUST PATIENCE

IF IT'S TOO GOOD TO BE TRUE, IT
PROBABLY ISN'T

IF YA GOT A ONE-TRACK MIND, MAKE SURE IT
DOESN'T JUMP BOTH RAILS

SOMETIMES A FELLER JUST PLAIN FORGETS
WHAT HE'S SUPPOSED TO REMEMBER

STRESS CAN BE CAUSED BY YER INABILITY TO
STOMP A MUD HOLE IN THE THING THAT'S
BUGGIN' YA

IT PAYS TO KEEP YER *HEAD OUT OF YER ASS*

THOSE WHO EXCEL HAVE THE DRIVE OF A
DYNAMO

PROFITABLE YEARS IN THE CATTLE BUSINESS
ARE AS SCARCE AS
HEN'S TEETH

THERE SHOULD BE A GOVERNMENT GRANT
TO FIGGER OUT THE MATING HABITS OF
THE COMMON CLOTHES HANGER

DON'T JUST STAND AROUND WITH YER ROPE
IN YER HAND

YOUNG MARRIED FOLKS SHOULD CONSIDER
RAISIN' THEIR GRANDKIDS FIRST, THEY'RE A
LOT MORE FUN THAN YER KIDS

ALWAYS DO YER BUSINESS DEALS IN YER *OWN*
BALL PARK

YA CAN GET A LOT MORE OUTA LIFTIN'
THAN PUSHIN'

IT CAN BE MIGHTY PRODUCTIVE TO FILE THE
CORNERS OFF YER *PILLS* BEFORE SHOOTIN'
THEM TO YER MEN

A SMILE IS AN INEXPENSIVE WAY TO
IMPROVE YER LOOKS

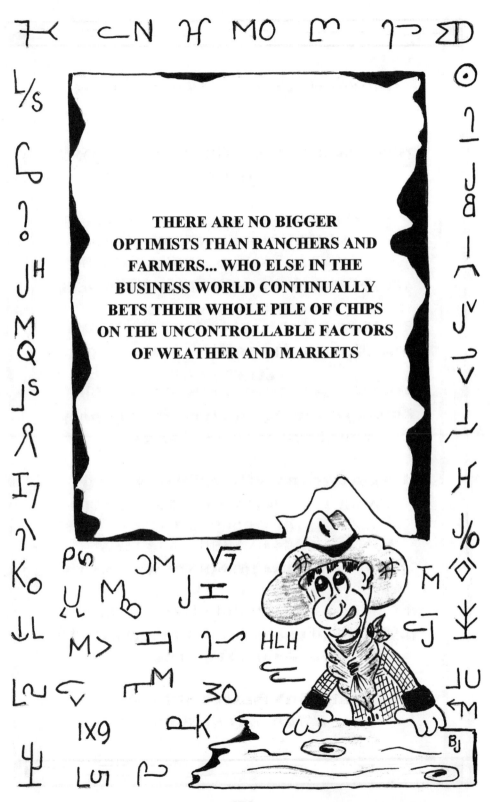

THERE ARE NO BIGGER OPTIMISTS THAN RANCHERS AND FARMERS... WHO ELSE IN THE BUSINESS WORLD CONTINUALLY BETS THEIR WHOLE PILE OF CHIPS ON THE UNCONTROLLABLE FACTORS OF WEATHER AND MARKETS

PRODUCTION FROM A BUREAUCRACY IS
SLOWER THAN A SNAIL ON CRUTCHES

IF I'D KNOWN I WAS GONNA LIVE THIS LONG,
I'D A TAKIN' BETTER CARE OF MYSELF

IF IT WALKS LIKE A DUCK AND SOUNDS LIKE A
DUCK, IT MUST BE A DUCK

ACCEPT YER DEFEATS WITH YER HEAD HELD
HIGH AND YER EYES OPEN

TIME IS ONE OF THE MOST VALUABLE THINGS
A FELLER'S GOT

CHILDREN ARE LIKE WATER... THEY CHOOSE
THE ROUTE OF LEAST RESISTANCE

TRYIN' TO GET A CATTLE RANCHER TO
CHANGE OCCUPATIONS IS LIKE TRYIN' TO
STOP A BULL FIGHT

THERE IS NO FUNCTIONAL EQUIVALENT TO
THE CATTLE BUSINESS

GEMINIS AND VIRGOS HAVE BEEN KNOWN TO
MAKE A HELLUVA TEAM

WHEN YA GET TO *CHOMPIN' AT THE BIT...* JUST
HOLD A TIGHT ASS....

IT MUST BE THE CHALLENGE THAT KEEPS A
COWMAN GOIN'... IT SURE AS HELL ISN'T THE
DRIVE OF SENSIBLE ECONOMICS

FOOL ME ONCE, SHAME ON YOU...
FOOL ME TWICE, SHAME ON ME....

NO ONE EVER GOT RICH LOOKIN' AT THE
GROUND DIRECTLY IN FRONT OF HIM

THERE'S NOT A HELLUVA LOT OF DIFFERENCE
BEWEEN RISK AND OPPORTUNITY

WHEN THINGS GO TO HELL... JUST BOW YER
NECK AND TRY HARDER

WHILE YOU'RE BUSY STOMPIN' OUT THE
PISS ANTS, BE CAREFUL THE ELEPHANTS DON'T
RUN OVER YA

MAKES YA WONDER IF COMPUTER
TECHNOLIGISTS SHOULD HOLLER *CALF ROPE*
NOW THAT THEY HAVE DEVELOPED MACHINES
THAT DO BUSINESS IN *NANO SECONDS*
(IF THE DANGED THINGS BURP, WE'LL BE
RUINED!)

A COWBOY WOULD JUST AS SOON GO
WITHOUT HIS PANTS AS TO GO WITHOUT HIS
HAT

A BANKER IS A FELLA WHO WILL LOAN YA HIS *SLICKER* ON A SUNNY DAY, THEN WANT IT BACK DAMN QUICK WHEN IT STARTS TO SPRINKLE

WHEN THE BALL IS IN YER COURT, BE SURE YA DON'T DOUBLE DRIBBLE

A COWMAN KNOWS HIS COWS SO WELL HE COULD RECOGNIZE THEIR ASHES IN A WHIRLWIND

THE LORD GIVETH... THE GOVERNMENT TAKETH AWAY

WHEN A COWBOY IS TOLD BY HIS BOSS TO TEND THE *BOVINES*... HE KNOWS HE HAS HIRED ON WITH THE WRONG OUTFIT

CATTLE RANCHIN' IS LIKE A GAME OF HORSESHOES, YA CAN GET A LITTLE SOMETHIN' FER BEIN' CLOSE

IF THE LORD HAD INTENDED FOR *CITY SLICKERS* TO VIEW A SUNRISE, HE WOULDA SCHEDULED IT FOR LATER IN THE DAY

MOST *DUDES* ON A COW RANCH DON'T LAST AS LONG AS A SNOW BALL IN HELL

IT TAKES MORE THAN INTENTIONS TO BE
PRODUCTIVE

DON'T HANG A COWBELL ON YER TROUBLES

IT'S A WEALTHY MAN WHO CAN TAKE A LEAK
IN HIS OWN BACK YARD

SOME LIVESTOCK BRAND INSPECTORS AND
TRUCK DRIVERS HAVE CAUSED MORE
ECONOMIC CHAOS FOR THE COWMAN THAN
TAXATION

IT MIGHT PAY TO PULL OUTA THE FAST LANE
IF YA KEEP GETTIN' REAR-ENDED

IF SOME POLITICIANS HAVE THEIR WAY,
GUESS WE BETTER LEARN HOW TO RAISE
CATTLE LIKE CHICKENS

THE MOST IMPORTANT PIECE OF EQUIPMENT
FOR A COWBOY WRITIN' A
BOOK IS AN ERASER

YOU'VE *HUBBED A STUMP* WHEN YA IGNORE
MOTHER NATURE

WHAT HAPPENS WHEN THE HUMAN BODY
IS SUBMERGED IN WATER?
THE TELEPHONE RINGS!

THE GREATEST ECONOMIC INDICATOR YA GOT
IS THE AMOUNT OF MONEY IN YER WALLET

DON'T GET IN A RUT, CAUSE THAT'S JUST A
GRAVE WITH THE ENDS KNOCKED OUT

LOOKS LIKE WE'RE GONNA HAVE TO START
THINNIN' OUT HUMANS IF WE'RE GONNA SAVE
THE ENVIRONMENT

RIGHT'S RIGHT AND WRONG'S WRONG AND
EVERYONE KNOWS THE DIFFERENCE

BEFORE YA GET TO THE *END OF YER ROPE,*
THROW A COUPLE *DALLIES* AROUND
YER *GUTS*

IT'S DOUBTFUL IF IT PAYS TO JUST *CRAWL
UNDER A ROCK*

WHEN YA *PULL LEATHER,* BE DAMN SURE YA
GET A HANDFULL

THREE MAIN THINGS KEEP A FELLER IN THE
COW BUSINESS; A STIFF UPPER LIP, A HARD
HEAD, AND LOTS OF *BACK BONE*

REAL ESTATE SUBDIVISIONS IN COW COUNTRY
ARE ABOUT AS POPULAR AS A PIT BULL
ON A SHORT LEASH

THE BEST ADVICE FOR A FELLER WHO
MAKES A THREAT IS TO TELL HIM NOT
TO LET THE DOOR KNOB HIT
HIM IN THE BUTT

SOME IMMATURE COWBOYS ARE
WILDER THAN OUTHOUSE RATS

"WHEN THEY'RE FAT, SELL 'EM" IS ONE OF
THE BEST GUIDES A COWMAN
CAN USE IN MARKETING HIS PRODUCT

WHEN YER CATTLE BUYER PROPOSES A
SLIDE CONTRACT FOR THE PURCHASE OF
YER CATTLE, THINK ABOUT *CAVEAT VENDER*

IT'S DOUBTFUL OUR FOREFATHERS COULD
HAVE SETTLED THE WEST WITHOUT RAWHIDE
AND BALIN' WIRE

WHEN THE BOSS CONTINUALLY RUNS ON A
FULL HEAD OF ADRENALIN... HE SURE IS HARD
TO FOLLOW

THE COLOR OF A BEEF ANIMAL IS ONLY
COSMETIC

IT'S A PITY SCIENCE CAN'T COME UP WITH A
PRESERVATION FOR THE VITALITY OF YOUTH

DON'T JUDGE A FELLER UNTIL YOU'VE
WALKED A MILE IN HIS BOOTS

WHEN YA APPROACH THE HIVE... BE CAREFUL
YA DON'T GET STUNG

JUST BECAUSE IT'S A MATTER OF PRINCIPLE
SHOULDN'T KEEP YA FROM BENDIN' A LITTLE

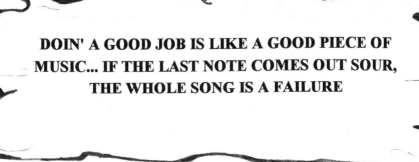

DOIN' A GOOD JOB IS LIKE A GOOD PIECE OF
MUSIC... IF THE LAST NOTE COMES OUT SOUR,
THE WHOLE SONG IS A FAILURE

THERE'S THREE MAIN THINGS A MAN OWES
HIS KIDS:
1. TEACH 'EM TO WORK AND WORK HARD
2. BUY ALL THE SCHOOLING THEY WILL TAKE
3. SHOW 'EM WHERE THE BIG OL' WORLD IS
AND SAY, "SIC 'EM"

SELLIN' CATTLE WITH A *SLIDE* PROVISION IN
THE CONTRACT MAKES NO MORE SENSE THAN
SHOOTIN' CRAPS IN LAS VEGAS

IT'S HARD TO IMAGINE HOW A MAN CAN FEEL
EXPRESSIVE WHEN HIS ONE AND ONLY SLANG
TERM IS "COTTON PICK IT"... BUT HE IS
HONORED FOR IT

COWBOYS MUST HAVE POINTED HEADS...
WHAT ELSE COULD BE THE SECRET TO THEIR
KEEPING A FOUR-INCH BRIM HAT ON IN A
HIGH WIND

YA SELDOM TAKE FULL MEASURE OF WHAT
YA GOT 'TIL AFTER YOU'VE LOST SOME OF IT

AS LONG AS CONGRESS KEEPS COMIN' OUT
WITH SOME TRUE HUMOR... WE HAVE SOME
HOPE

PLENTY OF RAIN WILL KEEP A COWMAN
CHEWIN' HIS CUD

SUCCESS IS SOMETHIN' DREAMS ARE MADE OF

GRASS IS THE ONLY THING A COWMAN
HAS TO SELL

IT DOESN'T HURT TO PUSH 'TIL YOU'VE WORN
A RUT IN THE GROUND

WHEN YOU'RE ON FINAL APPROACH, BE
SURE YER WHEELS ARE DOWN

IT'S TIME TO TURN IN YOUR RING AND YER TIE TACK WHEN YA CAN'T GET ALONG WITH THE HIGHER COMMAND

WHEN A FELLER DOES YA A *GOOD TURN...* BE SURE YA DANCE AT HIS WEDDING

ONE OF THE MOST IMPORTANT PIECES OF EQUIPMENT A COWBOY CAN HAVE AT THE HORSE CORRAL IN THE MORNING IS A LANTERN

TRYIN' TO *HEEL* SOMETHIN' WITH A LIMBER ROPE IS JUST ABOUT AS BAD AS TRYIN' TO BRAND WITH A COLD BRANDIN' IRON

BE SURE YA ALWAYS KNOW WHICH WAY THE WIND IS BLOWING

A COWMAN STAYS IN THE BUSINESS 'CAUSE HE PLAIN CAN'T TURN LOOSE

BE SURE YER GUN'S LOADED BEFORE YOU GO HUNTING

MOST PEOPLE WHO THINK THEY ARE FAMILIAR WITH THE OUTDOORS, DON'T KNOW WHETHER A COW SLEEPS ON THE GROUND OR ROOSTS IN A TREE

WHEN YER *IN A TIGHT,* LET YER HORSE
HAVE HIS HEAD

DRAG DRIVERS ARE LIKE THE TAIL OF A DOG

THE BEST WAY TO RUIN A FELLER IS TO KEEP
GIVIN' HIM THINGS

CATTLE MARKET PREDICTORS AND WEATHER
FORCASTERS ARE A LOT ALIKE... THEY
REALLY DON'T KNOW

SUCCESS COMES FROM THE THREE D's...
DESIRE... DETERMINATION... DEDICATION....

YOU KNOW YER HITTIN' THE BALL WHEN
YOU'VE SEEN AS MANY PRETTY SUNRISES AS
YOU HAVE PRETTY SUNSETS

DON'T GET MAD... GET EVEN

YOU KNOW A COWBOY IS GETTING OLD WHEN
HIS STIRRUPS START GETTING LONGER

OLD COWBOYS DON'T DIE... THEY JUST KEEP
SADDLIN' OLD HORSES

YA KNOW YOU'RE GETTIN' OLD WHEN YA
SQUAT TO RISE AND BAKE ON
THE SQUAT

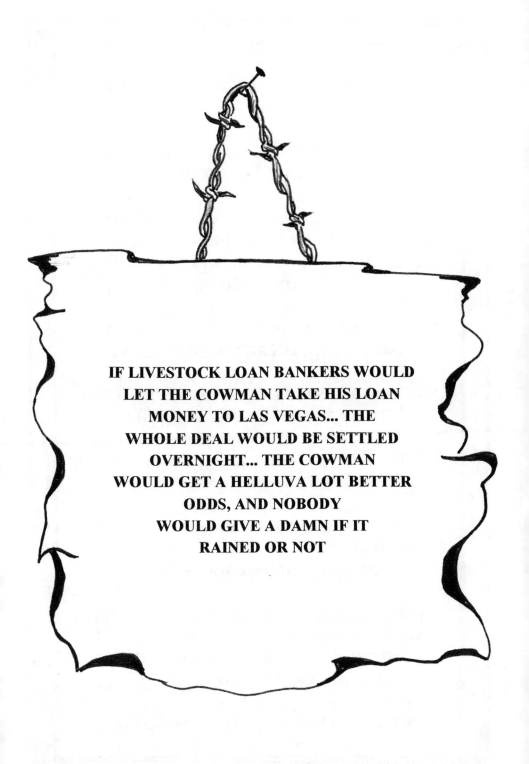

IF LIVESTOCK LOAN BANKERS WOULD
LET THE COWMAN TAKE HIS LOAN
MONEY TO LAS VEGAS... THE
WHOLE DEAL WOULD BE SETTLED
OVERNIGHT... THE COWMAN
WOULD GET A HELLUVA LOT BETTER
ODDS, AND NOBODY
WOULD GIVE A DAMN IF IT
RAINED OR NOT

WHEN YA QUIT TRYIN' TO GO... YA WITHER UP
AND FADE AWAY

WHEN YER NET WORTH GETS AS BIG AS YER
PHONE NUMBER, YA GOT 'ER MADE

YA CAN SURE GET *ON THE HOOK* WHEN YOU'VE
HOED YER OWN ROW, AND THEN COME ACROSS
A FELLER THAT'S AS WORTHLESS AS A BUMP
ON A LOG

CLIMBIN' TO THE TOP OF THE LADDER IS ONE
THING, STAYIN' THERE IS SOMETHIN' ELSE

SOME FELLERS WILL COMPLAIN EVEN WHEN
THEY'RE HUNG WITH A NEW ROPE

TO GIVE A TOUGH JOB A *LICK AND A PROMISE* IS
BETTER THAN NOTHING AT ALL

A FELLER AT 65 THAT SAYS HE CAN DO AS
MUCH AS HE DID AT 35 SURE WAS A *SORRY*
SUCKER WHEN HE WAS YOUNG

WHEN A RANCHER GOES TO A LIVESTOCK
AUCTION AND HAS A SURPLUS OF FEED AT
HOME, HE BECOMES JUST LIKE A KID IN A
CANDY STORE

NOTHING VENTURED, NOTHING GAINED

**THE ROMANCE OF PUNCHIN' COWS SURE IS
ABSENT WHEN ALL OF THE HORSES
IN YER MOUNT ARE**
KNOT HEADED

LOYALTY CAN'T BE BOUGHT, IT'S ONLY GIVEN

**THE COWMAN, LOW MAN ON THE
TOTEM POLE, ALWAYS**
SUCKS THE HIND TIT

DON'T EVER GET IN A SPOT WHERE YA GET
EARED DOWN

**COWBOYS ARE VISIONARIES... PERIPHERAL
THAT IS**

**IT SELDOM PAYS TO WANDER AROUND BEHIND
LITTLE ANIMALS**

**AN ECONOMIST IS AN ACCOUNTANT WITHOUT
A SENSE OF HUMOR**

THERE'S NO LOVE LIKE TRUE LOVE

**I COULDN'T 'A GOT 'ER DONE WITHOUT
T.L.A'S "LITTLE BLACK BOOK"**

**WHEN YOU'RE NEEDIN' A PLACE TO ROOST,
PULL INTO THE** *WAGON YARD*

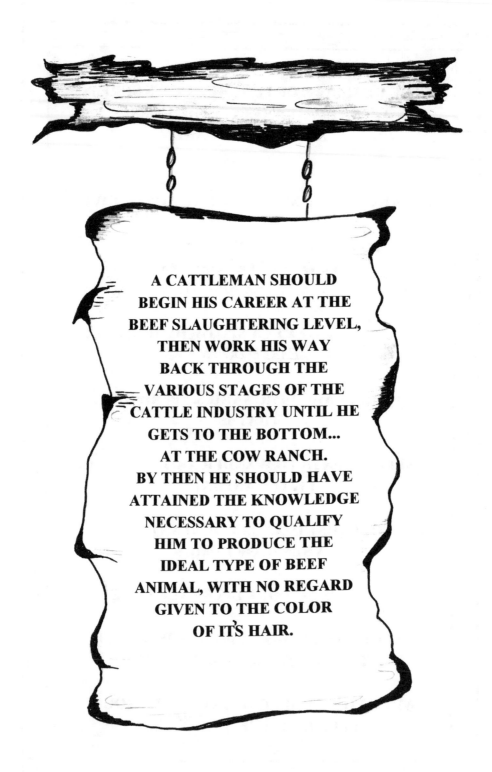

A CATTLEMAN SHOULD
BEGIN HIS CAREER AT THE
BEEF SLAUGHTERING LEVEL,
THEN WORK HIS WAY
BACK THROUGH THE
VARIOUS STAGES OF THE
CATTLE INDUSTRY UNTIL HE
GETS TO THE BOTTOM...
AT THE COW RANCH.
BY THEN HE SHOULD HAVE
ATTAINED THE KNOWLEDGE
NECESSARY TO QUALIFY
HIM TO PRODUCE THE
IDEAL TYPE OF BEEF
ANIMAL, WITH NO REGARD
GIVEN TO THE COLOR
OF IT'S HAIR.

Glossary

**DON'T ROPE ANYTHING YA
CAN'T GET YER ROPE
OFF OF....**

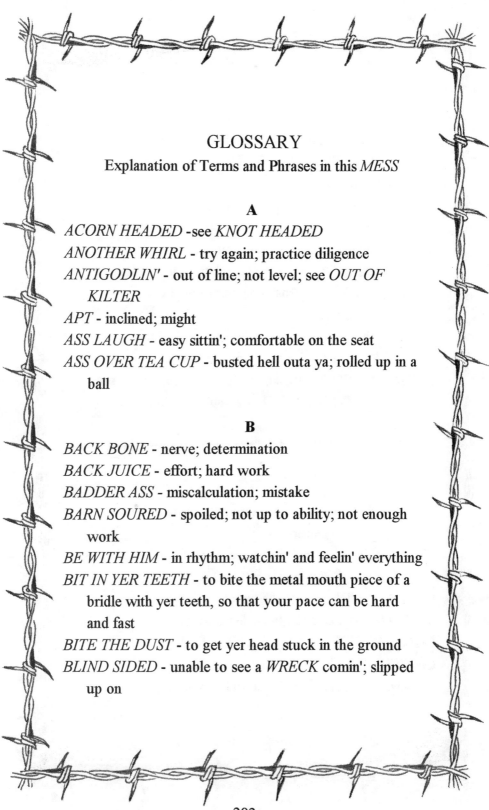

GLOSSARY
Explanation of Terms and Phrases in this *MESS*

A

ACORN HEADED -see *KNOT HEADED*

ANOTHER WHIRL - try again; practice diligence

ANTIGODLIN' - out of line; not level; see *OUT OF KILTER*

APT - inclined; might

ASS LAUGH - easy sittin'; comfortable on the seat

ASS OVER TEA CUP - busted hell outa ya; rolled up in a ball

B

BACK BONE - nerve; determination

BACK JUICE - effort; hard work

BADDER ASS - miscalculation; mistake

BARN SOURED - spoiled; not up to ability; not enough work

BE WITH HIM - in rhythm; watchin' and feelin' everything

BIT IN YER TEETH - to bite the metal mouth piece of a bridle with yer teeth, so that your pace can be hard and fast

BITE THE DUST - to get yer head stuck in the ground

BLIND SIDED - unable to see a *WRECK* comin'; slipped up on

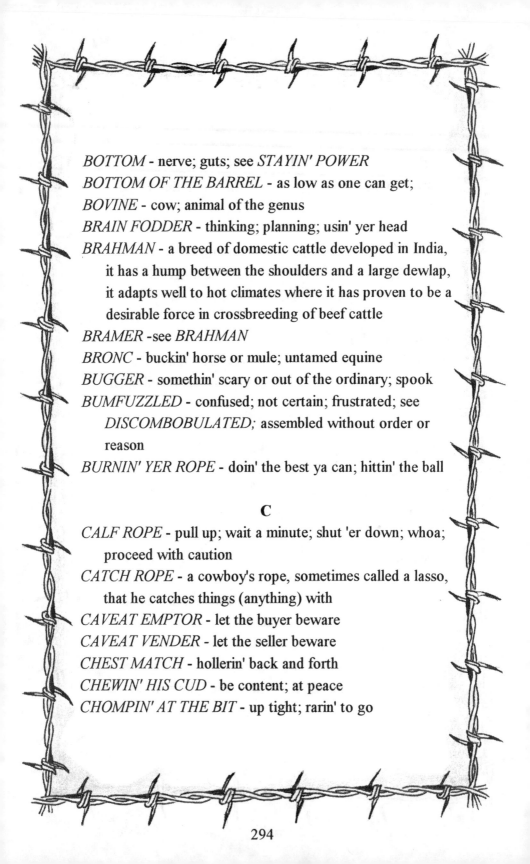

BOTTOM - nerve; guts; see *STAYIN' POWER*

BOTTOM OF THE BARREL - as low as one can get;

BOVINE - cow; animal of the genus

BRAIN FODDER - thinking; planning; usin' yer head

BRAHMAN - a breed of domestic cattle developed in India, it has a hump between the shoulders and a large dewlap, it adapts well to hot climates where it has proven to be a desirable force in crossbreeding of beef cattle

BRAMER -see *BRAHMAN*

BRONC - buckin' horse or mule; untamed equine

BUGGER - somethin' scary or out of the ordinary; spook

BUMFUZZLED - confused; not certain; frustrated; see *DISCOMBOBULATED;* assembled without order or reason

BURNIN' YER ROPE - doin' the best ya can; hittin' the ball

C

CALF ROPE - pull up; wait a minute; shut 'er down; whoa; proceed with caution

CATCH ROPE - a cowboy's rope, sometimes called a lasso, that he catches things (anything) with

CAVEAT EMPTOR - let the buyer beware

CAVEAT VENDER - let the seller beware

CHEST MATCH - hollerin' back and forth

CHEWIN' HIS CUD - be content; at peace

CHOMPIN' AT THE BIT - up tight; rarin' to go

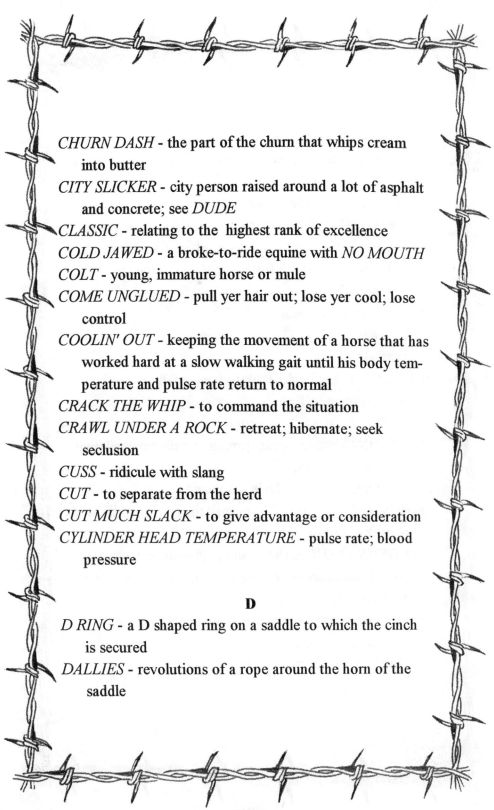

CHURN DASH - the part of the churn that whips cream into butter

CITY SLICKER - city person raised around a lot of asphalt and concrete; see *DUDE*

CLASSIC - relating to the highest rank of excellence

COLD JAWED - a broke-to-ride equine with *NO MOUTH*

COLT - young, immature horse or mule

COME UNGLUED - pull yer hair out; lose yer cool; lose control

COOLIN' OUT - keeping the movement of a horse that has worked hard at a slow walking gait until his body temperature and pulse rate return to normal

CRACK THE WHIP - to command the situation

CRAWL UNDER A ROCK - retreat; hibernate; seek seclusion

CUSS - ridicule with slang

CUT - to separate from the herd

CUT MUCH SLACK - to give advantage or consideration

CYLINDER HEAD TEMPERATURE - pulse rate; blood pressure

D

D RING - a D shaped ring on a saddle to which the cinch is secured

DALLIES - revolutions of a rope around the horn of the saddle

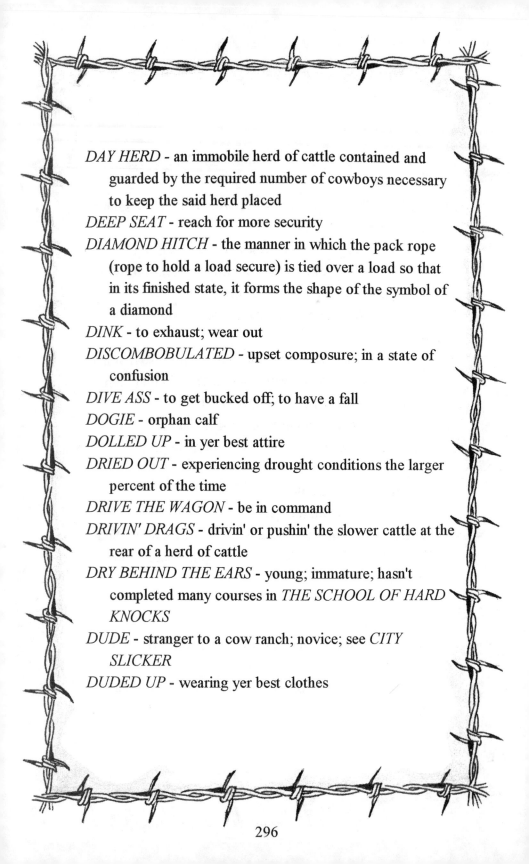

DAY HERD - an immobile herd of cattle contained and
guarded by the required number of cowboys necessary
to keep the said herd placed

DEEP SEAT - reach for more security

DIAMOND HITCH - the manner in which the pack rope
(rope to hold a load secure) is tied over a load so that
in its finished state, it forms the shape of the symbol of
a diamond

DINK - to exhaust; wear out

DISCOMBOBULATED - upset composure; in a state of
confusion

DIVE ASS - to get bucked off; to have a fall

DOGIE - orphan calf

DOLLED UP - in yer best attire

DRIED OUT - experiencing drought conditions the larger
percent of the time

DRIVE THE WAGON - be in command

DRIVIN' DRAGS - drivin' or pushin' the slower cattle at the
rear of a herd of cattle

DRY BEHIND THE EARS - young; immature; hasn't
completed many courses in *THE SCHOOL OF HARD
KNOCKS*

DUDE - stranger to a cow ranch; novice; see *CITY
SLICKER*

DUDED UP - wearing yer best clothes

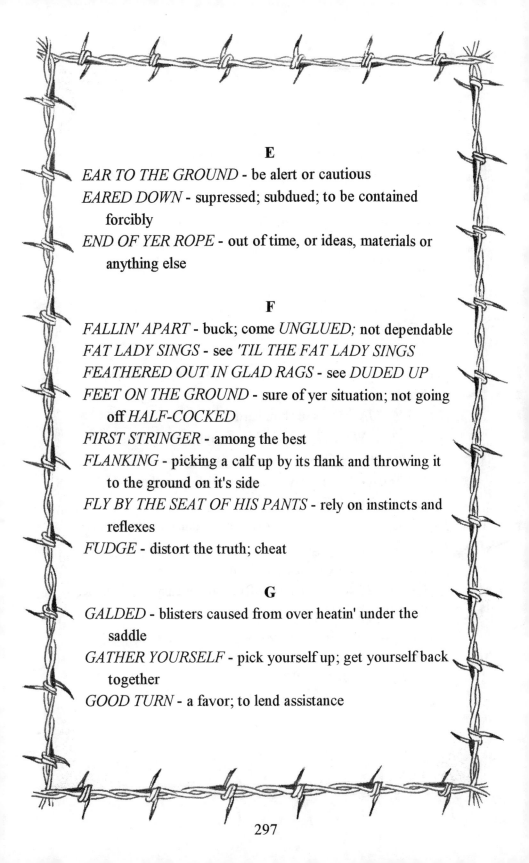

E

EAR TO THE GROUND - be alert or cautious

EARED DOWN - supressed; subdued; to be contained
forcibly

END OF YER ROPE - out of time, or ideas, materials or
anything else

F

FALLIN' APART - buck; come *UNGLUED;* not dependable

FAT LADY SINGS - see *'TIL THE FAT LADY SINGS*

FEATHERED OUT IN GLAD RAGS - see *DUDED UP*

FEET ON THE GROUND - sure of yer situation; not going
off *HALF-COCKED*

FIRST STRINGER - among the best

FLANKING - picking a calf up by its flank and throwing it
to the ground on it's side

FLY BY THE SEAT OF HIS PANTS - rely on instincts and
reflexes

FUDGE - distort the truth; cheat

G

GALDED - blisters caused from over heatin' under the
saddle

GATHER YOURSELF - pick yourself up; get yourself back
together

GOOD TURN - a favor; to lend assistance

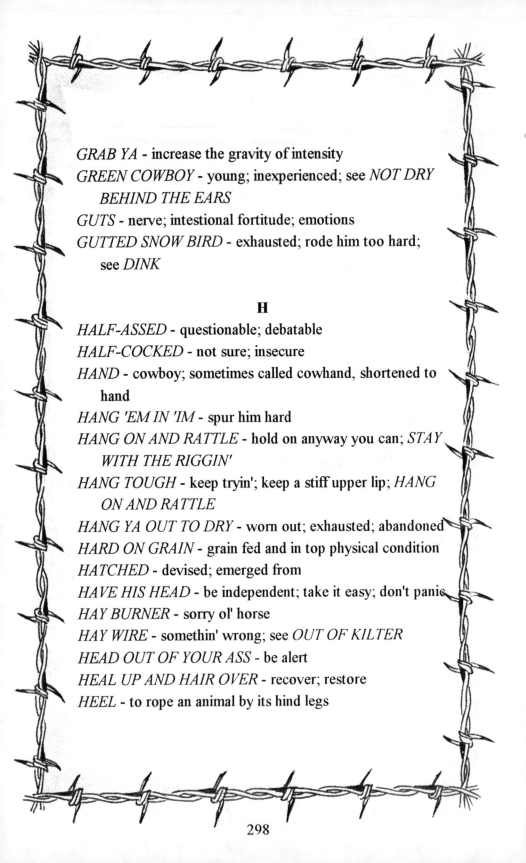

GRAB YA - increase the gravity of intensity

GREEN COWBOY - young; inexperienced; see *NOT DRY BEHIND THE EARS*

GUTS - nerve; intestional fortitude; emotions

GUTTED SNOW BIRD - exhausted; rode him too hard; see *DINK*

H

HALF-ASSED - questionable; debatable

HALF-COCKED - not sure; insecure

HAND - cowboy; sometimes called cowhand, shortened to hand

HANG 'EM IN 'IM - spur him hard

HANG ON AND RATTLE - hold on anyway you can; *STAY WITH THE RIGGIN'*

HANG TOUGH - keep tryin'; keep a stiff upper lip; *HANG ON AND RATTLE*

HANG YA OUT TO DRY - worn out; exhausted; abandoned

HARD ON GRAIN - grain fed and in top physical condition

HATCHED - devised; emerged from

HAVE HIS HEAD - be independent; take it easy; don't panic

HAY BURNER - sorry ol' horse

HAY WIRE - somethin' wrong; see *OUT OF KILTER*

HEAD OUT OF YOUR ASS - be alert

HEAL UP AND HAIR OVER - recover; restore

HEEL - to rope an animal by its hind legs

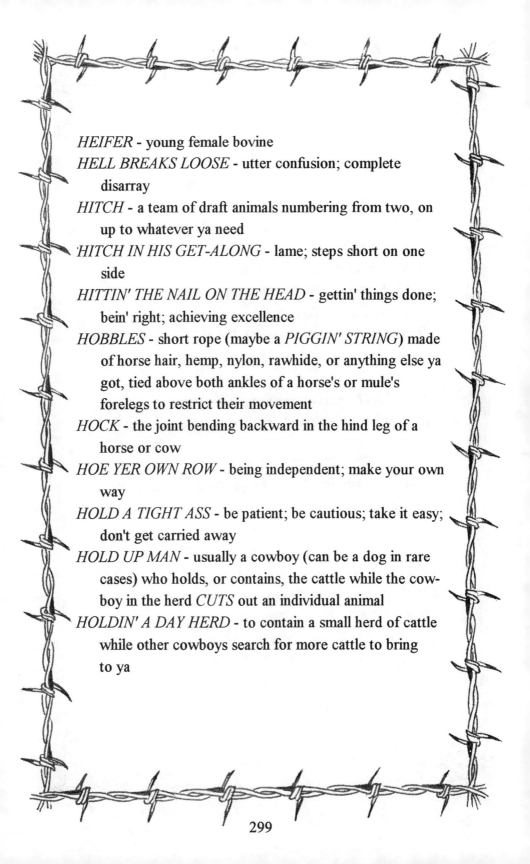

HEIFER - young female bovine

HELL BREAKS LOOSE - utter confusion; complete disarray

HITCH - a team of draft animals numbering from two, on up to whatever ya need

HITCH IN HIS GET-ALONG - lame; steps short on one side

HITTIN' THE NAIL ON THE HEAD - gettin' things done; bein' right; achieving excellence

HOBBLES - short rope (maybe a *PIGGIN' STRING*) made of horse hair, hemp, nylon, rawhide, or anything else ya got, tied above both ankles of a horse's or mule's forelegs to restrict their movement

HOCK - the joint bending backward in the hind leg of a horse or cow

HOE YER OWN ROW - being independent; make your own way

HOLD A TIGHT ASS - be patient; be cautious; take it easy; don't get carried away

HOLD UP MAN - usually a cowboy (can be a dog in rare cases) who holds, or contains, the cattle while the cowboy in the herd *CUTS* out an individual animal

HOLDIN' A DAY HERD - to contain a small herd of cattle while other cowboys search for more cattle to bring to ya

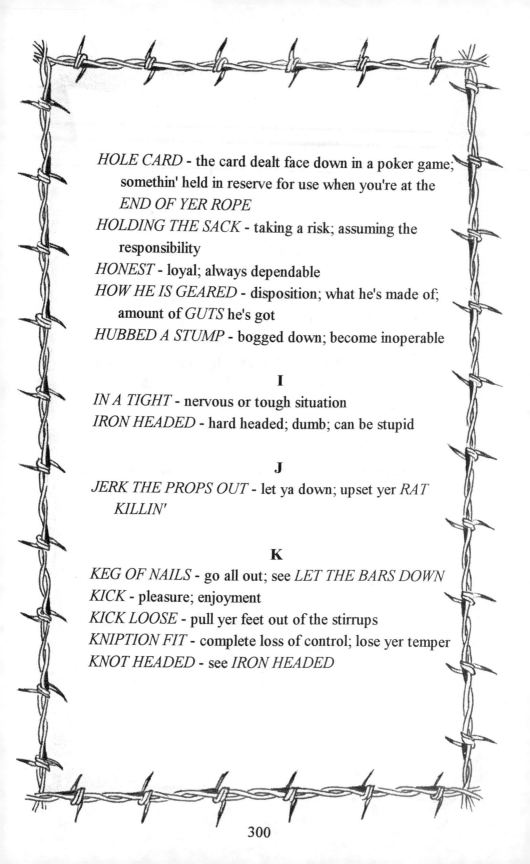

HOLE CARD - the card dealt face down in a poker game; somethin' held in reserve for use when you're at the *END OF YER ROPE*

HOLDING THE SACK - taking a risk; assuming the responsibility

HONEST - loyal; always dependable

HOW HE IS GEARED - disposition; what he's made of; amount of *GUTS* he's got

HUBBED A STUMP - bogged down; become inoperable

I

IN A TIGHT - nervous or tough situation

IRON HEADED - hard headed; dumb; can be stupid

J

JERK THE PROPS OUT - let ya down; upset yer *RAT KILLIN'*

K

KEG OF NAILS - go all out; see *LET THE BARS DOWN*

KICK - pleasure; enjoyment

KICK LOOSE - pull yer feet out of the stirrups

KNIPTION FIT - complete loss of control; lose yer temper

KNOT HEADED - see *IRON HEADED*

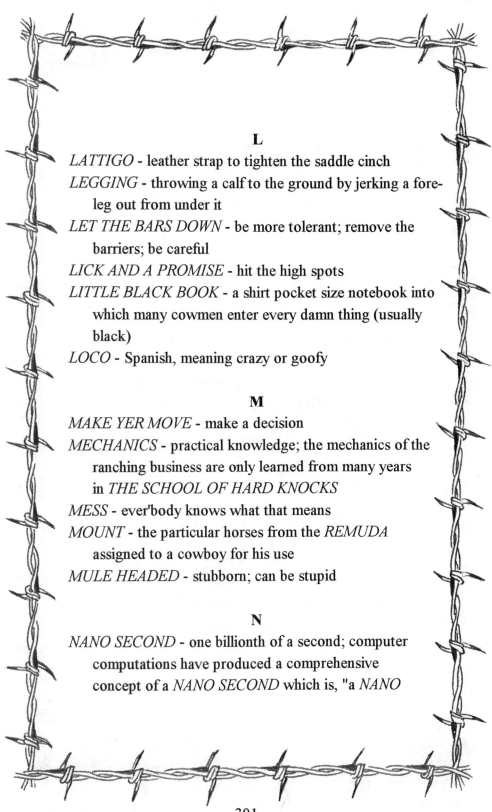

L

LATTIGO - leather strap to tighten the saddle cinch

LEGGING - throwing a calf to the ground by jerking a fore-leg out from under it

LET THE BARS DOWN - be more tolerant; remove the barriers; be careful

LICK AND A PROMISE - hit the high spots

LITTLE BLACK BOOK - a shirt pocket size notebook into which many cowmen enter every damn thing (usually black)

LOCO - Spanish, meaning crazy or goofy

M

MAKE YER MOVE - make a decision

MECHANICS - practical knowledge; the mechanics of the ranching business are only learned from many years in *THE SCHOOL OF HARD KNOCKS*

MESS - ever'body knows what that means

MOUNT - the particular horses from the *REMUDA* assigned to a cowboy for his use

MULE HEADED - stubborn; can be stupid

N

NANO SECOND - one billionth of a second; computer computations have produced a comprehensive concept of a *NANO SECOND* which is, "a *NANO*

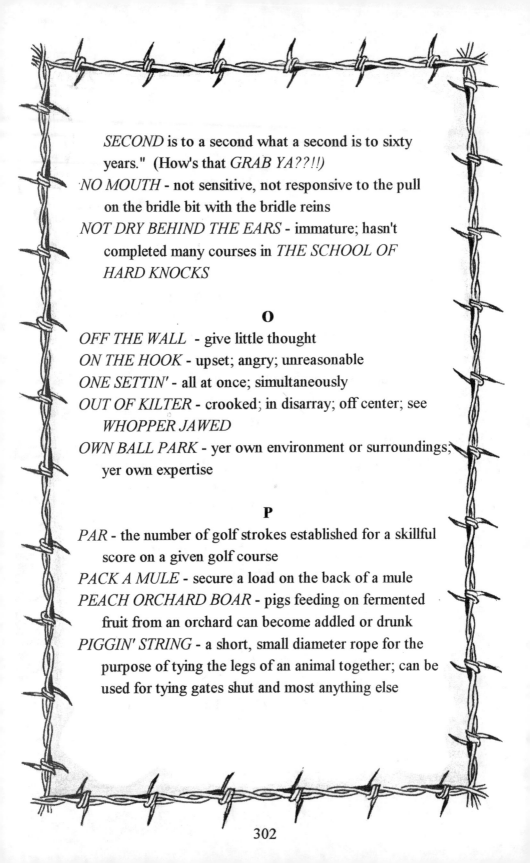

SECOND is to a second what a second is to sixty
   years." (How's that *GRAB YA??!!)*

NO MOUTH - not sensitive, not responsive to the pull
   on the bridle bit with the bridle reins

NOT DRY BEHIND THE EARS - immature; hasn't
   completed many courses in *THE SCHOOL OF
   HARD KNOCKS*

O

OFF THE WALL - give little thought

ON THE HOOK - upset; angry; unreasonable

ONE SETTIN' - all at once; simultaneously

OUT OF KILTER - crooked; in disarray; off center; see
   WHOPPER JAWED

OWN BALL PARK - yer own environment or surroundings;
   yer own expertise

P

PAR - the number of golf strokes established for a skillful
   score on a given golf course

PACK A MULE - secure a load on the back of a mule

PEACH ORCHARD BOAR - pigs feeding on fermented
   fruit from an orchard can become addled or drunk

PIGGIN' STRING - a short, small diameter rope for the
   purpose of tying the legs of an animal together; can be
   used for tying gates shut and most anything else

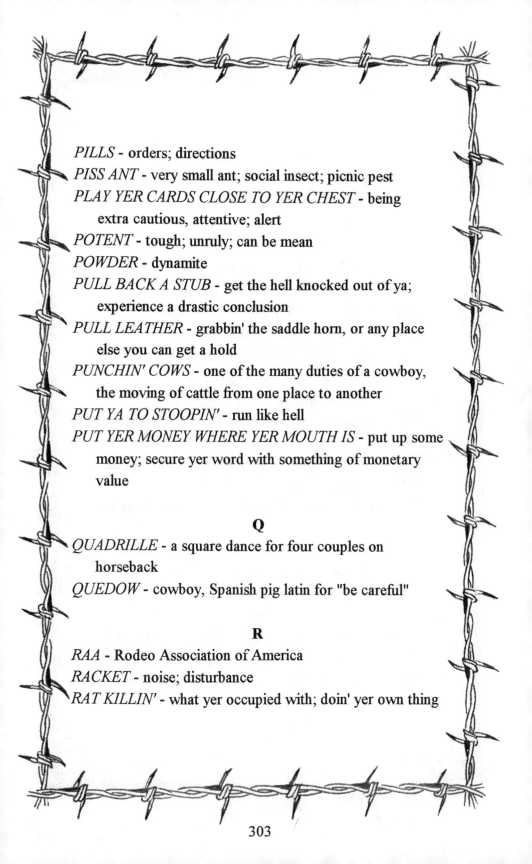

PILLS - orders; directions

PISS ANT - very small ant; social insect; picnic pest

PLAY YER CARDS CLOSE TO YER CHEST - being extra cautious, attentive; alert

POTENT - tough; unruly; can be mean

POWDER - dynamite

PULL BACK A STUB - get the hell knocked out of ya; experience a drastic conclusion

PULL LEATHER - grabbin' the saddle horn, or any place else you can get a hold

PUNCHIN' COWS - one of the many duties of a cowboy, the moving of cattle from one place to another

PUT YA TO STOOPIN' - run like hell

PUT YER MONEY WHERE YER MOUTH IS - put up some money; secure yer word with something of monetary value

Q

QUADRILLE - a square dance for four couples on horseback

QUEDOW - cowboy, Spanish pig latin for "be careful"

R

RAA - Rodeo Association of America

RACKET - noise; disturbance

RAT KILLIN' - what yer occupied with; doin' yer own thing

303

RATTLE A MAN'S CAGE - get a feller's attention

RATTLE AROUND - runnin' around loose; things not
    secured

RATTLED - upset; discomposed

RAWHIDE - untanned cowhide

RAZOO - trouble; cattle tryin' to run away

*REINFORCEMENT OF VOCAL SOUNDS BY
    SYMPATHETIC VIBRATION* - resonance

REMUDA - herd of ranch saddle horses

REP - a cowboy from the neighboring ranch representing
    the said ranch's brand

RIGGIN' - your equipment

ROOT ROT - ignore where ya came from; forget yer
    heritage

ROUGH UNDER THE COLLAR - mean; cantankerous

ROUND ASS - insecurity on horseback

ROWEL - a sharp toothed wheel inserted into the end of a
    SPUR

RUNNIN' BACKWARDS - not standin' by yer word or not
    doin' what you said you would do; not *STANDIN' PAT*

S

SACK OUT - part of the process of gentling and breaking
    a horse or mule by hitting it with a gunny sack, saddle
    blanket, coat, *SLICKER,* or other non-injurious flexible
    items

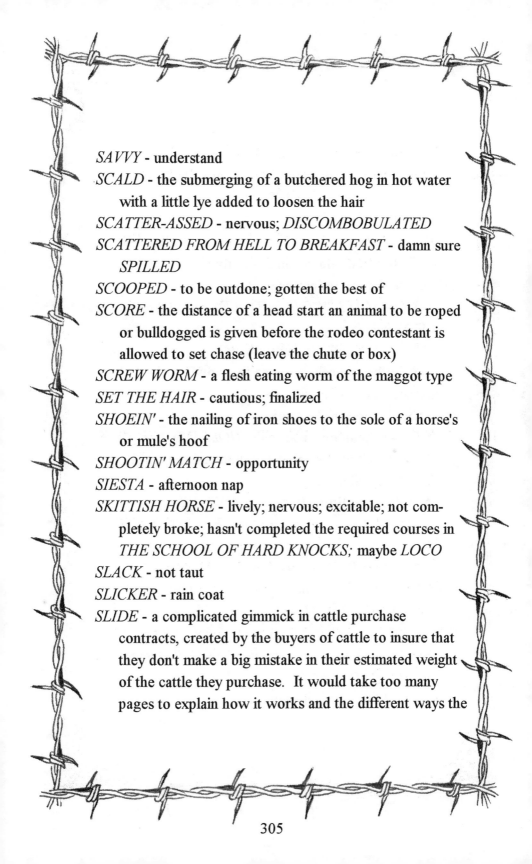

SAVVY - understand

SCALD - the submerging of a butchered hog in hot water
with a little lye added to loosen the hair

SCATTER-ASSED - nervous; *DISCOMBOBULATED*

SCATTERED FROM HELL TO BREAKFAST - damn sure
SPILLED

SCOOPED - to be outdone; gotten the best of

SCORE - the distance of a head start an animal to be roped
or bulldogged is given before the rodeo contestant is
allowed to set chase (leave the chute or box)

SCREW WORM - a flesh eating worm of the maggot type

SET THE HAIR - cautious; finalized

SHOEIN' - the nailing of iron shoes to the sole of a horse's
or mule's hoof

SHOOTIN' MATCH - opportunity

SIESTA - afternoon nap

SKITTISH HORSE - lively; nervous; excitable; not completely broke; hasn't completed the required courses in
THE SCHOOL OF HARD KNOCKS; maybe *LOCO*

SLACK - not taut

SLICKER - rain coat

SLIDE - a complicated gimmick in cattle purchase
contracts, created by the buyers of cattle to insure that
they don't make a big mistake in their estimated weight
of the cattle they purchase. It would take too many
pages to explain how it works and the different ways the

final monies are computed. And then too, this author doesn't really understand all he knows about the contract, but it is a *CLASSIC!*

SMOKE SETTLE - be calm

SON-OF-A-BITCH - no good sucker; aggravating imbecile

SORRY - bad; unbearable; no good; rotten

SPILL - to scatter; to lose control

SPITTOON STAYS IN THE MIDDLE - don't take your eyes off the subject

SPOILED - disobedient; hard to handle

SPURS - spiked wheels strapped to a cowboy's heels and used to urge his horse forward

SQUIRRELY - eccentric; crazy

STAKED - helping out financially; *HOLDING THE SACK*

STAMPEDE - complete chaos; to bolt and run in fear; total loss of organization

STAND PAT - be firm; *HOLD A TIGHT ASS*

STAY WITH THE RIGGIN' - do your best; take a *DEEP SEAT;* see *HANG ON AND RATTLE*

STAYIN' POWER - determination; unwavering ability

STEAL A RIDE - being uneasy or overly cautious; *HOLDING A TIGHT ASS*

STEER HORSE - a horse used in the rodeo event of steer roping, trained to jerk cattle down and hold them on the end of a *CATCH ROPE*

STICK OF POWDER - dynamite

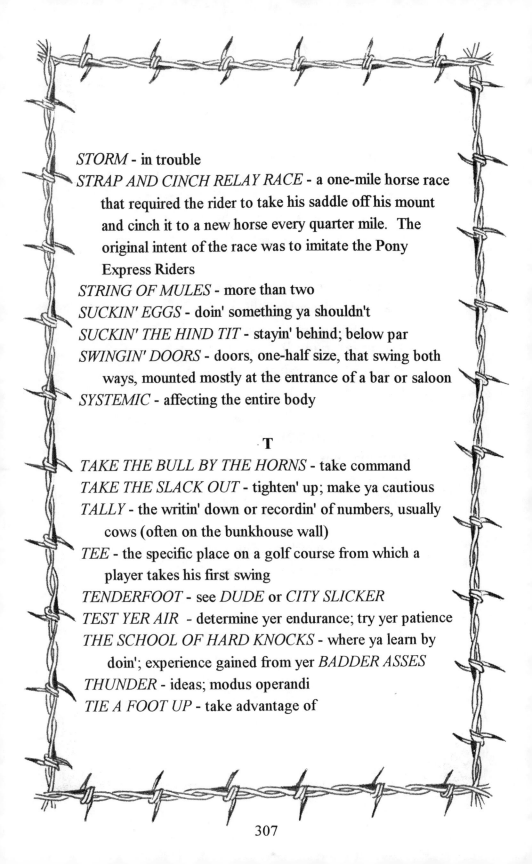

STORM - in trouble

STRAP AND CINCH RELAY RACE - a one-mile horse race
that required the rider to take his saddle off his mount
and cinch it to a new horse every quarter mile. The
original intent of the race was to imitate the Pony
Express Riders

STRING OF MULES - more than two

SUCKIN' EGGS - doin' something ya shouldn't

SUCKIN' THE HIND TIT - stayin' behind; below par

SWINGIN' DOORS - doors, one-half size, that swing both
ways, mounted mostly at the entrance of a bar or saloon

SYSTEMIC - affecting the entire body

T

TAKE THE BULL BY THE HORNS - take command

TAKE THE SLACK OUT - tighten' up; make ya cautious

TALLY - the writin' down or recordin' of numbers, usually
cows (often on the bunkhouse wall)

TEE - the specific place on a golf course from which a
player takes his first swing

TENDERFOOT - see *DUDE* or *CITY SLICKER*

TEST YER AIR - determine yer endurance; try yer patience

THE SCHOOL OF HARD KNOCKS - where ya learn by
doin'; experience gained from yer *BADDER ASSES*

THUNDER - ideas; modus operandi

TIE A FOOT UP - take advantage of

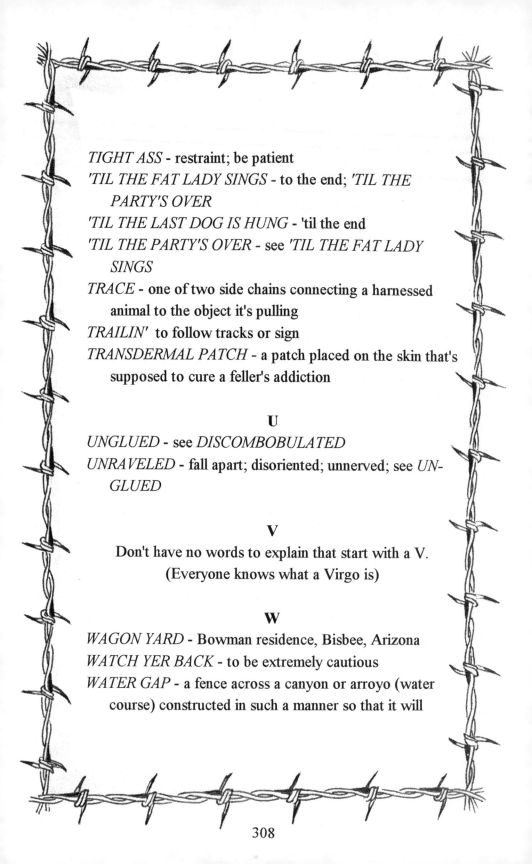

TIGHT ASS - restraint; be patient

'TIL THE FAT LADY SINGS - to the end; *'TIL THE PARTY'S OVER*

'TIL THE LAST DOG IS HUNG - 'til the end

'TIL THE PARTY'S OVER - see *'TIL THE FAT LADY SINGS*

TRACE - one of two side chains connecting a harnessed animal to the object it's pulling

TRAILIN' to follow tracks or sign

TRANSDERMAL PATCH - a patch placed on the skin that's supposed to cure a feller's addiction

U

UNGLUED - see *DISCOMBOBULATED*

UNRAVELED - fall apart; disoriented; unnerved; see *UNGLUED*

V

Don't have no words to explain that start with a V.
(Everyone knows what a Virgo is)

W

WAGON YARD - Bowman residence, Bisbee, Arizona

WATCH YER BACK - to be extremely cautious

WATER GAP - a fence across a canyon or arroyo (water course) constructed in such a manner so that it will

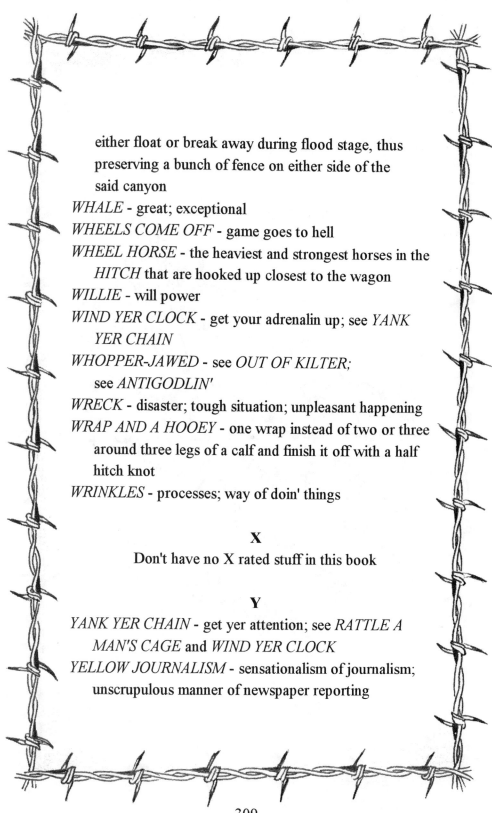

either float or break away during flood stage, thus preserving a bunch of fence on either side of the said canyon

WHALE - great; exceptional

WHEELS COME OFF - game goes to hell

WHEEL HORSE - the heaviest and strongest horses in the *HITCH* that are hooked up closest to the wagon

WILLIE - will power

WIND YER CLOCK - get your adrenalin up; see *YANK YER CHAIN*

WHOPPER-JAWED - see *OUT OF KILTER*; see *ANTIGODLIN'*

WRECK - disaster; tough situation; unpleasant happening

WRAP AND A HOOEY - one wrap instead of two or three around three legs of a calf and finish it off with a half hitch knot

WRINKLES - processes; way of doin' things

X
Don't have no X rated stuff in this book

Y
YANK YER CHAIN - get yer attention; see *RATTLE A MAN'S CAGE* and *WIND YER CLOCK*

YELLOW JOURNALISM - sensationalism of journalism; unscrupulous manner of newspaper reporting

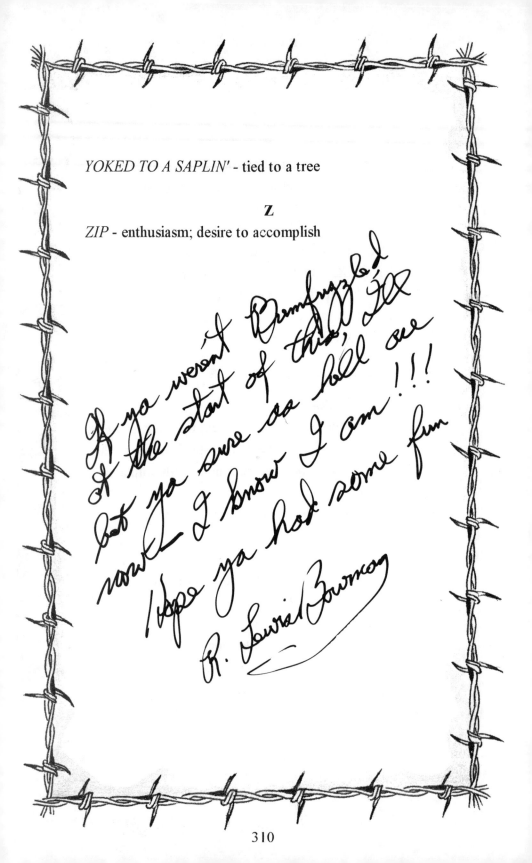

YOKED TO A SAPLIN' - tied to a tree

Z

ZIP - enthusiasm; desire to accomplish

If ya weren't Bumfuzzled
At the start of this, I'll
bet ya sure as hell are
now! I know I am!!!
Hope ya had some fun

R. Louis Bowman

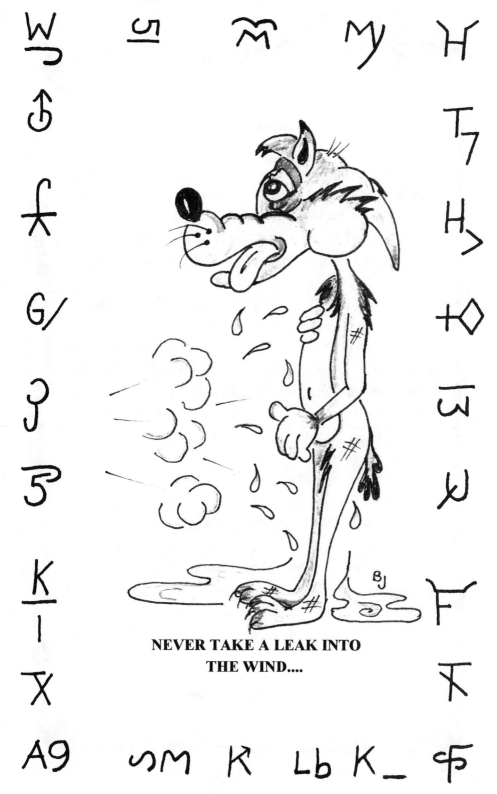

**NEVER TAKE A LEAK INTO
THE WIND....**

EPILOGUE

It's my book, BUT..... this *BUMFUZZLED* mess never would have been *HATCHED* without the talents, diligence, and dedication of B. J. Kuykendall, my editor and cartoonist, her husband Tom, my computer and lay-out man, and their daughter Tammy Smith, my co-editor and artist.

For being ol' *DRIED OUT* fourth and fifth generation Arizona cow ranchers, (the sixth is now on the ground) my crew did a *WHALE* of a job. It looks to me like they missed their calling.... people with these kinds of abilities shouldn't waste them on a danged ol' cow! However, their cattle are non-debatable as being among the very best in the south-western U.S.. It's amazing how some folks just naturally excel at whatever they do. My heart-felt thanks and appreciation is extended to these folks.

IT'S BEEN A LONG OLE TRAIL BUT THERE SURE HAVE BEEN SOME SCENIC SPOTS ALONG THE WAY. Sure hope some of you got a *KICK* out of this, but if not, I can't apologize 'cause we sure had a helluva lot of fun putting it together; and it **KEPT US AWAY FROM THOSE** *SWINGIN' DOORS!*

Here's wishing all of you greener pastures and bigger calf crops.

R. Lewis Bowman

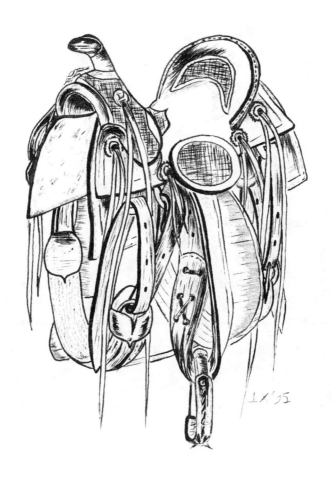

YA LEARN SOMETHIN' WITH
EVERY GOODBYE

**ALWAYS DO WHAT YA HAVE TO DO... THE LAST
FOUR LETERS OF AMERICAN SPELL
"I CAN"**

The Author
←

R. Lewis Bowman
1995

THE AUTHOR

R. Lewis Bowman made his appearance on this good
earth in the year 1924 at Old San Carlos (Arizona); which
has been under water for sixty-seven years due to the
construction of Coolidge Dam. (Editors Note: We could
have a lot of fun with this fact, but guess we'd better let
sleepin' dogs lie!)

The "full scoop" of the author's early years has not been
totally revealed to this crew, but we're sure he was whippin'
and spurrin' from the moment of conception.

Lewis grew up in San Carlos, Arizona (formerly known
as Rice on Highway 60.) He attended grammar school
there, and high school in Globe, Arizona. Mr. B learned
multiple "R's" (including ridin', ropin' and reasonin' with a
bunch of stubborn cows in his spare time). From the time
he was five years old, he was a "pro rodeo man"; travelin'
the circuit for ten years, whenever possible, with uncles Ed,
Everett, and Skeet.

Our author did a short stint at the University of Arizona
(Tucson, Arizona) before World War II. He was in the
U.S. Army Air Corp from 1943 - 1946 as an aerial
navigator on B-17's and a flight engineer on B-29's.

No matter how many opportunities knock on your door,
it's the determined (and lucky) man who can apply his
experience and "savvy" to the life he loves, Lewis did just

that.

1946 offered a partnership in the Hook and Line Ranch (Coolidge Dam). Hard work, and doin' what you're born to do seem to make the impossible possible. We hope some of the family photos capture the essence of this statement.

1948 brought R. Lewis Bowman the love of his life; Barbie consented to be the best partner he'd ever hope to have. (He had been courtin' her since age eight). Two impressive sons came from that union; David Bowman, M.D. and Doug Bowman, an educator of handicapped children. They in turn, have added their families to the Bowman legacy. This family extension includes four special grand-children. (Just ask Lewis; he'll tell you!)

From 1950 - 1956 our author and his family joined Steve Bixby and his registered hereford outfit in Globe, Arizona.

Willcox, Arizona, Betty Lane and the JJ Lane Estate offered a continuence in the cattle business for the next four years. During this period of time (in 1957) R. Lewis Bowman made history by having the first herd of polled Charlois cattle in the U.S.A. This outstanding bunch of cattle was taken to the Bill Stevenson SO Ranch, which was leased by the Bowmans from 1960- 1973.

While leasing the ranch, Lewis continued his diversity in many fields; which included being a Cochise County Deputy under Sheriff Phil Olander in Willcox, Arizona. Jim Willson was the "Naco Deputy" during this period of time. What a

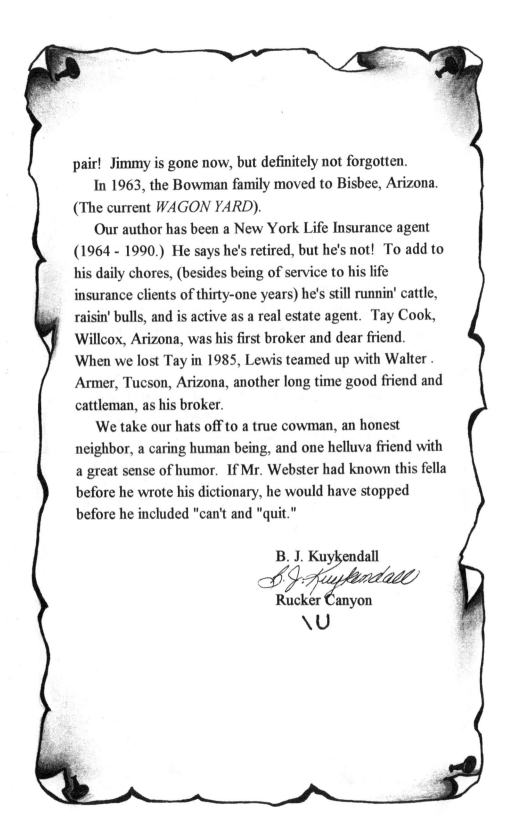

pair! Jimmy is gone now, but definitely not forgotten.

In 1963, the Bowman family moved to Bisbee, Arizona. (The current *WAGON YARD*).

Our author has been a New York Life Insurance agent (1964 - 1990.) He says he's retired, but he's not! To add to his daily chores, (besides being of service to his life insurance clients of thirty-one years) he's still runnin' cattle, raisin' bulls, and is active as a real estate agent. Tay Cook, Willcox, Arizona, was his first broker and dear friend. When we lost Tay in 1985, Lewis teamed up with Walter . Armer, Tucson, Arizona, another long time good friend and cattleman, as his broker.

We take our hats off to a true cowman, an honest neighbor, a caring human being, and one helluva friend with a great sense of humor. If Mr. Webster had known this fella before he wrote his dictionary, he would have stopped before he included "can't and "quit."

B. J. Kuykendall

B. J. Kuykendall

Rucker Canyon

\U